U0115803

Units in Cogtse Rgyalrong Discourse:

Prosody and Grammar

嘉戎語卓克基話的話語研究：韻律與語法

You-Jing Lin 林幼菁————著

ISBN 978-986-478-349-6

Front cover image by Pusamam Digital Culture CO.,LTD.
Printed by Beltom Technology Corp.

First Printing, 2020.04

WAN JUAN LOU BOOKS CO., Ltd.
6F.-3, No. 41, Sec. 2, Roosevelt Rd.,
Da'an Dist.,Taipei City 106, Taiwan
Tel (02)23216565　FAX (02)23218698
service@wanjuan.com.tw

作　　者　林幼菁
責任編輯　呂玉姍
特約校稿　曾貴祺
發 行 人　林慶彰
總 經 理　梁錦興
總 編 輯　張晏瑞
封面設計　菩薩蠻數位文化有限公司
印　　刷　百通科技股份有限公司
發　　行　萬卷樓圖書(股)公司
　　　　　臺北市羅斯福路二段 41 號 6 樓之 3
　　　　　電話 (02)23216565 傳真 (02)23218698
　　　　　電郵 SERVICE@WANJUAN.COM.TW
ISBN 978-986-478-349-6
2020 年 7 月初版二刷
2020 年 4 月初版
定價：新臺幣 480 元

TABLE OF CONTENTS

.

ACKNOWLEDGEMENTS

I am indebted to the Rgyalrong people with whom I worked and lived in the field. Prominent among them is my primary consultant, Dongfang Yang, a highly gifted and conscientious speaker of the Cogtse dialect of Rgyalrong. I thank him for sharing his expertise with unending patience, humor and insight. I also want to thank several other speakers for participating in this research by recording narratives: Rɟamtsʰo əlrɟɐltʃû, Songlin Wang, Yulan Gao, Yezhen Lu, and Atʃâm Kərʒi. While I was exploring the wonders of the language in the field, I was aided tremendously by the support and hospitality of my Rgyalrong friends, who generously accepted me as a member of the big Rgyalrong family. In particular, I would like to thank Dongfang Yang, his wife Mtshomoscit, and his aunt Nɐrwumtshu for their warm and loving care. Because of them, the Rgyalrong Area has become a second home for me.

With the deepest gratitude, I would like to thank Carol Genetti and Jackson T. -S Sun for their scholarship on Sino-Tibetan languages and linguistics, as well as for their advice, support, encouragement and warm care. I can't be prouder to say that my accomplishments as a scholar are due in large part to their guidance. I would like to thank Marianne Mithun and

Sandy Thompson for showing me the marvels of grammar in discourse; and I also wish to thank Jonathan Evans and Matthew Gordon for all the feedback and in-depth discussions regarding my research of Rgyalrong prosody.

Ard I thank Dexter, for helping me pursue my dream by providing unwavering support, encouragement and unconditional love.

ABSTRACT

Units in Cogtse Rgyalrong Discourse: Prosody and Grammar

by

You-Jing Lin

This study examines units of prosody and grammar in Cogtse Rgyalrong (henceforth Cogtse), a Tibeto-Burman language spoken by Rgyalrong Tibetans in southwestern Sichuan, China. The present study explores how naturally occurring speech flow is organized into basic prosodic units in this language, and examines the grammatical taxonomy of these units. It is the first extensive research on prosody and grammar based on real-time speech in Rgyalrong, as well as the first study of tone and intonation in a language that has a privative tonal system of zero versus falling tone.

The analysis of Cogtse word prosody reveals that the language has a privative tonal system in which falling tone contrasts with zero. Tonal assignment is critically dependent on the metrical parsing of words into feet.

The analysis of Cogtse intonation, on the other hand, involves three phonological features, namely phrasal rules, prosodic accent, and the boundary tone H%. Together these facts argue for a multi-layered model of prosodic structure that incorporates the syllable, word, foot, prosodic phrase, and intonation unit as domains for distinct yet interacting rules.

Cogtse speech can be organized into IUs using related prosodic cues, the reliability of which has been confirmed by inter-rater reliability tests.

The IUs are then coded for structural type. The distribution of these structural types shows that the preferred syntactic structure of the Cogtse IU is the clause. A surprisingly high proportion of multi-clausal IUs (31%) does not follow the "one clause per IU" tendency as observed by Chafe (1980) in English. Nonetheless, it has been shown that most of these seemingly anomalous cases could be accounted for by the proximity principle of iconicity, as well as strong links of rhetorical relations between the clauses within a multi-clausal IU.

Chapter 1
General Introduction

1.0. Introduction

The present project 'Units in Cogtse Rgyalrong Discourse: Prosody and Grammar' examines units of prosody and grammar in Cogtse Rgyalrong spontaneous narratives. In this study, prosody is characterized by auditory aspects of speech including duration, pitch, and loudness. The present project aims to explore how naturally occurring speech flow is organized into basic prosodic units in this language, and to examine the grammatical taxonomy of these units. It will be the first extensive research on Rgyalrong prosody and grammar, as well as the first study of intonational patterns in a language that has a privative tonal system.

This detailed analysis of Rgyalrong prosody and grammar will be the first study that adopts a discourse-functional approach to investigate real-time speech of Rgyalrong, a language subgroup in the Sino-Tibetan family. The studies on Rgyalrong languages have reported many unique and important findings with respect to phonology, semantics, morphosyntax, and historical linguistics; and more and more related research is grounded on discourse data/texts rather than elicited materials. However, no research of naturally-occurring speech has been undertaken on this language subgroup. What underlies the present study is the observation that "the use of language to communicate in natural settings is fundamental to the organization of languages" (Hopper 1997), and thus "grammar codes best what speakers do most" (Du Bois 1985). I believe that by undertaking a detailed analysis of Rgyalrong spontaneous speech, we will be able to discover important aspects of the language that cannot be observed in elicited or isolated data.

This general introduction contains a brief overview of some of the major components that constitute the theoretical foundation and database of the present investigation. It starts with an introduction of the Rgyalrong language, the language under study in this research (§1.1). Section 0 discusses three major concepts that make up the prosodic analysis of the present study: the intonation unit (§1.2.1), intonation (§1.2.2), and the relationship between tone and intonation (§1.2.3). The theoretical background of the study of grammar in the IU will be discussed in §1.3. The general research questions the present project will address are summarized in §1.4. Section 1.5 contains detailed information on the data that are used in the present investigation. It provides a brief discussion of the types of data that were chosen to form the database of the study (i.e., spontaneous and non-elicited narratives for the analysis of prosody, and prosody and grammar, plus a small number of constructed examples for the study of tone-intonation relationships). Meanwhile, it describes the methodology used in data collection, as well as information about the participants, and the narratives collected and analyzed for this study. Finally, the organization of the whole book will be described in §1.6.

1.1. Cogtse Rgyalrong and Rgyalrongic Languages

The speech form examined for the present study is the Cogtse (or Zhuokeji 卓克基) dialect of Situ Rgyalrong, which belongs to the Rgyalrong group. The Rgyalrong group consists of four closely related but mutually unintelligible languages: Situ (四土), Japhug (茶堡), Tshobdun (草登), and Showu (used primarily in Rjong'bur 日部) (Jacques 2014a; Sun 2000a; Sun 2000b). The subgroups of Rgyalrong, Khroskyabs (Jacques et al. 2017), and Horpa (Sun 2015; Sun 2000b) in turn comprise the Rgyalrongic group under the so-called "Qiangic" branch (Sun et al. 2007) in the Sino-Tibetan family. Figure 1.1 is a Rgyalrongic Stammbaum created based on the subclassification as proposed by Jacques (2014a):

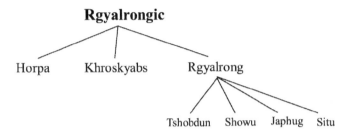

Figure 1. 1 Rgyalrongic Stammbaum as proposed by Jacques (2014) and
J. Sun (2015: 731)

Figure 1.2 illustrates the geographical distribution of these languages near and within 'Barkhams（马尔康）County in Rngaba (阿坝) Tibetan and Qiang Autonomous Prefecture, Sìchuān, China. Some other Rgyalrongic speech forms that have been investigated by linguists are not included in this map. They are used in neighboring areas in both Rngaba Prefecture and Dkarmjos (甘孜) Tibetan Autonomous Prefecture.

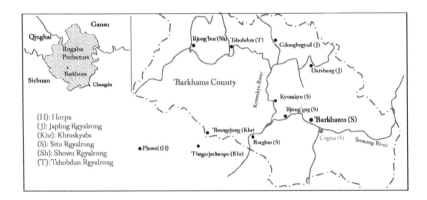

Figure 1. 2 The distribution of the Rgyalrong (four languages), Horpa and Khroskyabs groups within and near 'Barkhams County in Rngaba Prefecture, Sìchuān

Linguistic work on Rgyalrongic languages based on modern linguistic frameworks has been progressing significantly, thanks to the efforts of linguists who have devoted themselves to the investigation of different linguistic aspects in various Rgyalrongic languages. Full grammars have been published for the Cogtse dialect of Situ (X. Lin 1993), the Kyomkyo dialect of Situ (Prins 2016), Japhug (Jacques 2008), and the Wobzi dialect of Khroskyabs (Lai 2017). A lexicon (Ngag-dbang-Tshul-khrims et al. 2009), two dictionaries (Huang & Sun 2002; Jacques 2018), and a collection of fully-analyzed texts (Y. Lin 2016b) have been made available. J. Sun, Nagano, and Jacques et al provide grammatical sketches of Tshobdun (2003; 2017) Cogtse Situ (Nagano 2001; 2003), and Stau (Jacques et al. 2017), respectively. Other studies on phonological, morphological, syntactic and historical issues in Rgyalrong and other Rgyalrongic languages include (Gates 2014; Gong 2014; Hu 2016; Jacques 2010a; 2010b; 2012a; 2012b; 2012c; 2013a; 2013b; 2014a; 2014b; 2015a; 2015b; 2016; Kin 1957-58; Lai 2013; 2015; 2016; Lin 1983; Lin 2000; 2002; 2003; 2009a; 2009b; 2012; 2016a; 2017a; 2017b; Lin & Luo 2003; Lin et al. 2012; Qu 1983; 1984; 1990; Sun 1996; 1998; 2000a; 2007a; 2012; 2014; 2015; to appear; Sun et al. 2017; Sun 2000b; 2004; 2005a; 2005b; 2007b; 2007c; 2008; Sun 2002; Sun & Lin 2007; Tian & Sun 2016a; 2016b; Zhang 2016).

Scholars involved in the research of Rgyalrongic languages have come to rely more and more on collections of discourse data that have been painstakingly collected over the past 15-20 years. However, as of this writing, there has yet to be any systematic prosodic analysis of any Rgyalrong texts, let alone any discussion of intonational phonology and the correspondence between prosody and grammar in this language. It is partly against this backdrop that the present study aims to explicitly describe the nature of syntactic and prosodic exponents of IUs in Rgyalrong. Cogtse, the Rgyalrong dialect selected for the present research, boasts complex morphosyntax and a fascinating privatively-opposed tonal system (cf. Chapter 2). Given the unique nature of Rgyalrong (morpho-)syntax and prosody, the study provides a new perspective on contour patterns, prosodic segmentation, and grammar in discourse.

1.2. Prosody

The present study assumes that speech flow can be exhaustively segmented into intonation units. The prosodic analysis of the Cogtse narratives thus involves three timing cues (pause, final lengthening, anacrusis), two pitch-pattern cues (pitch reset, coherent intonation), and a voice quality cue (i.e., creakiness). More details about these cues are provided in §3.1.1. The following subsections will discuss the definition of the intonation unit (§1.2.1), how intonation is defined and analyzed in the present study (§1.2.2), as well as the relationship between tone and intonation (§1.2.3).

1.2.1. Intonation Unit (IU)

The intonation unit (henceforth IU) is defined in auditory terms. It is characterized by Chafe (1987) as "a sequence of words combined under a single, coherent intonation contour". It is analogous to the tone group (Halliday 1967), tone unit (Crystal 1969; Quirk et al. 1964), and intonational phrase (Nespor & Vogel 1986; Pierrehumbert 1980; Selkirk 1984), intonation-group (Cruttenden 1997), and prosodic unit (Genetti 2007a; Genetti & Slater 2004). Chafe (1987; 1994) characterizes the IU as the minimal unit of thought organization, and hypothesizes that the IU represents a speaker's focus of consciousness. Park (2002), incorporating this hypothesis into his research, demonstrates that the intonation unit is not only a unit of cognitive processing, but also a resource speakers can use and maneuver for achieving interactional goals.

Whereas many studies on discourse prosody establish their models on the basis of English data, a small number of discourse-based studies on IUs in other languages are available. These include Genetti and Slater (2004) on Dolakha Newar (in which the basic unit in prosody is termed the "prosodic unit" rather than the IU), Park (2001; 2002) on Korean, Matsumoto (2003) on Japanese, and Tao (1996) on Mandarin Chinese. In particular, Genetti and Slater (2004), while investigating Dolakha Newar (a Tibeto-Burman language spoken in Nepal), provide a rigorous methodology of speech segmentation and contour-type examination. Using a bottom-up approach, Genetti and Slater segment a long narrative into basic prosodic units, describe all the contour shapes observed in the data, and categorize them by their shared features. They are able to secure the reliability of their unit segmentation and contour categorization by high inter-transcriber agreement. The contour types are eventually coded by their functions with regard to transitional continuity. The methodology and research procedures demonstrated in these studies are very clear and thorough. They make a great model for those who study from scratch a prosodic system as previously undescribed.

1.2.2. Intonation

In the present study, I use the term "intonation" to refer to phonological structures of the phrase and utterance levels which are represented by specific pitch patterns. Intonation in this sense is close in spirit to what Ladd defines as "the use of suprasegmental phonetic features to convey 'postlexical' or sentence-level pragmatic meanings in a linguistically structured way" (1996).

Instead of regarding intonational contours as global shapes of slopes, the present study adopts many notions and elements of the autosegmental/metrical (AM) theory in describing the intonational patterns of Cogtse. Originally developed to account for English intonation (Beckman et al. 2005; Beckman & Hirschberg 1994; Liberman & Pierrehumbert 1984; Pierrehumbert 1980; Pitrelli et al. 1994; Silverman et al. 1992), the theory argues that pitch contours consist of local "events". It is proposed that overall contours over a phrase or sentence are the result of repeated local effects.

The theory has been applied to the analysis of intonation in languages other than English, including Japanese (Beckman & Pierrehumbert 1986; Pierrehumbert & Beckman 1988; Venditti 2005), Korean (Jun 2005a), Chickasaw (Gordon 2005), and Cantonese (Wong et al. 2005). The present study will provide another case study based on this framework. It will be demonstrated that Cogtse intonation can be sufficiently accounted for based on three phonological parameters: prosodic phrases, the prosodic accent, and the boundary tone.

1.2.3. Tone and Intonation

Cogtse is a (privative) tone language, therefore the issue of possible interactions between tone and intonation will also be addressed in the prosodic analysis. Tone is a phonological characteristic of lexical items and is largely fixed; whereas intonation, as Wennerstrom (2001: 47)observes, "can be altered depending on the discourse role played by the constituents with which tones are associated... Thus intonation has the greater potential to influence discourse meaning".

Three possible scenarios have been reported about the interaction between intonation and pitch-shape of the utterance-final word. The first possibility is that, at the utterance-final position, the original tonal value of the word is maintained. Garding and Svantesson (1994) report that in Lao tones are basically maintained in citation, carrier, question, phrase-final, and utterance-final contexts. Duration and pitch range, not intonation, are actually the most salient features that distinguish these contexts. Matisoff (1994) observes that Lahu does not use a rising contour for yes-no questions. He suggests that Lahu does not rely heavily on intonation to convey pragmatic meanings since the language has a rich array of sentence-final particles to do the job. In Thai, lexical tone of words in one-word statements remains the same as in citation (Luksaneeyanawin 1998).

The second possibility is that intonation can override tone. Beijing Chinese, as Kratochvil (1998) describes, exhibits "downward channeling" (i.e., declination) in declarative sentences, which even overrides the rising tone. The same situation is also reported by Dung et al. (1998) for Vietnamese. For Thai, according to Luksaneeyanawin (1998), words in one-word utterances of interrogatives and unfinished statements are all characterized by raised pitch and narrower pitch range, no matter what their lexical tone is.

The other possibility is that input tones are changed, but in such a way that tonal contrast is preserved. In Tanacross Athabaskan, for example, interrogative and imperative intonations affect the stem tone, but the tonal distinction is preserved in their pre-stem tone-spread constraints (Holton 2005).

Cogtse Rgyalrong has a privative tonal system in which /HL/ contrasts with /Ø/. The surface melodies of these contrastive tones can be altered by the interaction among the three phonological tones that determine the surface shape of intonational contours. Given the special nature of the Cogtse tone system, the present study will add a new case-study to the relatively limited range of studies on tone and intonation.

1.3. Grammar in the IU

In addition to exploring thoroughly the prosodic characteristics of the Cogtse IU, the present dissertation also aims to investigate its grammatical taxonomy. This will be the first grammatical profile of Cogtse from a discourse-based perspective. Discourse-functional linguists consider discourse as "the primary locus of grammar of the world's languages" (Cumming & Ono 1997). One crucial observation is that grammar is formed in, or emerges, from recurrent patterns of everyday use (Hopper 1995). Functional linguists have long figured that contexts often provide information that helps determine the function of a linguistic signal that may otherwise prove puzzling. Therefore, over the last three decades, discourse grammarians have been paying more and more time and attention to naturally-occurring data that demonstrate different contexts (Hopper 1995).

This research therefore proposes to study grammar based on IUs in discourse. It will first segment speech flow into IUs, and then look at possible grammatical correlates to these units. The related theoretical assumptions, including the issues of the preferred syntactic structure, the "one clause per IU" constraint, full vs. elliptic clauses, as well as the "one IU per clause" constraint as discussed in Chafe (1980; 1987; 1988; 1994; 1996; 1997; 1998), Tao(Tao 1996), Croft (1995), Matsumoto (2003) and Halliday (1967; 1985) will be reviewed. Based on related data discovered in Cogtse, the present study will address the issue of preferred syntactic structure, as well as the violation of the "one clause per IU" constraint as observed in this language.

1.4. General Research Questions

The general research questions the present study addresses are:

RQ1: How can the word-prosody system of Cogtse be characterized? Is it tonal, pitch-accented, or both?

RQ2: How does prosody organize speech into basic units?

RQ3: What are the contour shapes observed on the Cogtse IU? How are they best described?

RQ4: What is the relationship between tone and intonation?

RQ5: What are the grammatical exponents of Cogtse IUs? What does the distribution of the structural types tell us about the grammatical organization of Cogtse natural speech?

RQ6: Is there any salient correlation between grammatical structures and contour shapes?

1.5. The Data

1.5.1. Spontaneous Narratives and Constructed Examples

The primary data for this study will be a body of spontaneous narratives. These are naturally-occurring, unscripted speech, as opposed to spoken data that are read and fully prefabricated. In fact, both spontaneous conversations and narratives make apt data for this study. Both are produced in real time, with no opportunity for editing, and both provide a rich array of linguistic cues that signal language processing. The most crucial reason why the present research restricts its data type to narratives is to obtain a better quality of recording, which secures clear acoustic signals for boundary cues and contour shapes. In natural conversation, speaker overlap is frequent, and very often it can hinder an analyst in capturing the complete contour shape of an utterance. Given the fact that little is known about Rgyalrong prosody at this stage, studying prosody in monologue narratives is a necessary initial step. The results obtained from this study surely will form a solid foundation for studies of conversation, discourse analysis, language use, and real-time language processing.

In addition to providing spontaneous narratives, two Cogtse speakers (one male and one female) were also recorded reading constructed sentences. The data were used to figure out the possible realizations of the lexical tones in different utterance-internal positions, and in distinct contexts.

1.5.2. Data Collection and Consultants

The data collected for this project were collected in two fieldtrips to the Rgyalrong area in 2006 and 2007. The Rgyalrong participants in this project are all native speakers of Cogtse Rgyalrong, and have lived in the First Hamlet of Xisuo Village of Cogtse Township since they were born. They participated in the project on a voluntary basis. Table 1.1 below provides basic information about the participants in this project.

Consultant Name	Gender	Age
1. Atʃâm kərʒi	Female	65
2. Yezhen Lu	Female	63
3. Yulan Gao	Female	63
4. Rʄamtsʰo əlrʄɐltʃû	Male	83
5. Songlin Guo	Male	67
6. Dongfang Yang	Male	54

Table 1.1 List of Cogtse Rgyalrong participants in the project, including their name, gender and age (as in 2007)

All the participants except for Dongfang Yang were asked to freely contribute two to three stories of either folklore or their personal experiences. In total, 20 narratives were collected and analyzed, totaling ninety-one minutes and five seconds of recorded data. However, the contributions of each participant were not equal. In my fieldtrip in 2006, I started with analyzing possible patterns observed in the narratives Dongfang Yang contributed, then collected more narratives by additional participants to examine the occurrence of the patterns in my second fieldtrip to the Rgyalrong area in 2007. Therefore, a considerable number of the narratives (seven out of twenty) were contributed by Dongfang Yang, my main consultant; and the other thirteen narratives were contributed by the other five consultants. Table 1.2 summarizes the contribution of the participants.

Participant name	Number of narratives	Total duration (minute:second)
1. atʃâm kərʒi	3	10:15
2. Yezhen Lu	2	10:29
3. Yulan Gao	2	11:24
4. Rʒamtsʰo əlrʲɐltʃû	3	11:45
5. Songlin Wang	3	11:50
6. Dongfang Yang	7	35:22
Total	20	91:05

Table 1.2 Number of narratives and the corresponding total duration contributed by each participant

Recordings were made in a quiet room using a condenser microphone and either an ASUS laptop with a M-Audio pre-amplifier or a M-Audio Digital Recorder. My main consultant recorded his narratives alone in the room, while the other participants were recorded in the presence of my main consultant, and one or two other participants. The audience (if any) occasionally provided back-channel responses to make the story-telling go more smoothly. Table 1.3 below shows the number of narratives and the duration of the recordings contributed by each speaker. The total duration of each narrative ranges from fifty seconds to almost nine minutes.[1]

---

1 A number of the narratives (i.e. Narratives 01, 03, 05, 07, 08, 09, 10, 11, 15, 16, 17, 18, 19, 20) have been published as fully analyzed texts in Y. Lin (2016).

Narrative number	Topic	Total Duration	Participant Name
01	Fish in burnt water	00:50	Dongfang Yang
02	Farmer's work	04:23	Dongfang Yang
03	My father and hunting	05:43	Dongfang Yang
04	Childhood: Housework	06:03	Dongfang Yang
05	Childhood: Our dogs and hunting	03:54	Dongfang Yang
06	Childhood: Picking mushroom and other activities	05:31	Dongfang Yang
07	Runaway horses	08:58	Dongfang Yang
08	A lost man and ghosts	04:30	ɽʝamtsʰo əlrʝɐltʃû
09	Three sons and a bird named Shakalapongka	02:13	ɽʝamtsʰo əlrʝɐltʃû
10	Three sons and their pilgrimages to Lhasa	05:02	ɽʝamtsʰo əlrʝɐltʃû
11	Feasts by rich and poor families	04:04	Yulan Gaʋ
12	Three sisters and a beggar	07:20	Yulan Gao
13	Three sisters and a beggar	08:52	Yezhen Lu
14	The speaker's own health situation	01:37	Yezhen Lu
15	Two families of different destinies	03:35	Songlin Wang
16	A giant and his parents	03:36	Songlin Wang
17	An idiot's wedding night	04:39	Songlin Wang
18	Mother and son	04:58	atʃâm kərʒi

Narrative number	Topic	Total Duration	Participant Name
19	How to make a king bark like a dog	02:51	atʃâm kərʒi
20	The king who punished a river	02:26	atʃâm kərʒi

Table 1.3 Information of narratives in the database: Narrative number, major topic, and name of the participant who told the story

Meanwhile, although the present study is mainly based on spontaneous data, constructed examples were also collected for the study of word prosody, as well as tone-intonation interaction. The examples referred to in the discussion of word prosody (Chapter 2) were selected from data that had been collected for my previous research projects during 1999-2002. The elicitation of intonation patterns in controlled environments could shed light on the basic patterns of tone-intonation interaction. In the second fieldtrip, I also recorded elicited data in the following contexts:

1) yes-no interrogatives
2) content interrogatives
3) declaratives
4) citation forms
5) utterance medial elements
6) focused elements

1.6. The Organization of the Book

In addition to this introductory chapter, the remaining four chapters of this monograph are organized as follows.

Chapter 2 explicates word prosody in Cogtse. Crucially, it explores how pitch is used to convey lexical and grammatical meanings of words. It is proposed that underlyingly, Cogtse has a privative tonal system in which falling tone contrasts with zero. The tonal variations that define the prosodic phrase are presented after the main analysis of word prosody.

Chapter 3 provides a prosodic analysis of the IU, its segmentation and the intonational patterns. This chapter starts with the identification of IUs by means of six prosodic cues, then proceeds to an internal analysis of intonation contours within IUs thus identified.

Chapter 4 introduces the transcription conventions applied in this study before presenting a study of grammar based on IUs in Cogtse narratives. It examines the grammatical taxonomy of each IU segmented using the prosodic methodology introduced in Chapter 3. Six criteria are proposed for the coding of grammatical exponents of the IUs. This study also discovers the correlation between prosody and extrapropositional meanings, as well as an interesting correspondence between prosody and grammar in the quotative construction.

Chapter 5 summarizes the major findings and offers some suggestions for future research.

Chapter 2
Word Prosody

2.0. Introduction

This chapter explicates word prosody in Cogtse. Crucially, it explores how pitch is used to convey lexical and grammatical meanings of words. I start with a review of previous studies on Cogtse word prosody (§2.1).[1] In particular, the pros and cons of an analysis involving pitch-accent will be discussed (§2.2) before a strictly tonal analysis is introduced in § 2.3. In the latter analysis, I propose that underlyingly Cogtse has a privative system in which falling tone contrasts with zero. Section 2.1 discusses tonal interactions between prosodic words. The tonal variations are only observed on the phrase level and thus define the prosodic phrase. Section 2.2 summarizes and discusses the findings.

2.1. Previous Analyses of Cogtse Word Prosody

The linguistic significance of tone in Cogtse has gradually transitioned from being unnoticed to being highly recognized as linguists discover more and more related facts. While undertaking the earliest extensive studies on Cogtse, Nagano

---

[1] Readers are referred to J. Sun (2005a; 2007c) for surveys of tonality in other Rgyalrongic languages.

(1984: 160) and Qu (1984) dismiss tone as insignificant for the language. Seven years later, X. Lin (1993: 744-755) observes some lexical and grammatical differences that are signaled by changes of tonal values. In particular, he discovers disyllabic minimal pairs that contrast only in tone, as well as examples of verbs that have recourse to tonal variations to achieve present and past-tense inflection. These discoveries, however, did not prompt X. Lin to view Cogtse tone from a perspective that is drastically different from that of his predecessors. In a rather reserved manner, he proposes that the functions of tone he discovers in Cogtse could have resulted from language contact with the neighboring Kham Tibetan or Sichuan Chinese, and suggests that no evidence shows that Cogtse will develop into a full-fledged tone language.

A major contribution made by Hsieh (1999) to the study of Cogtse word prosody is that he provides the first systematic phonological account of Cogtse tonality. Grounded in tonal patterns observed in basic vocabulary, as shown below in (1), Hsieh proposes that non-derived and uninflected words in Cogtse show a binary word-tone system that contrasts High (/H/) and Falling (/HL/). Once the tonal value of the final syllable is specified, the tonal shape of the word is predictable.

(1) Surface tonal patterns of words on /H/ and /HL/

		1-syllable	2-syllable	3-syllable	4-syllable
/H/	:	**H**	**L-H**	**L-H-H**	**L-H-H-L**
/HL/	:	**HL**	**L-HL**	**L-H-HL**	**L-H-H-HL**

In addition to the lexical tones, Hsieh suggests that Cogtse has a pitch-accent system that is culminative and is defined by a pitch drop. Words like *kʰarʝalili* [L-H-H-L] 'swallow (bird)', therefore, can be analyzed as having an accent on the penultimate syllable since a pitch drop occurs from the penultimate to the final syllables.

(2) (Hsieh 1999: 155)

kʰarʝalili

Meanwhile, Hsieh also discovers grammatically-conditioned pitch-accent placement in the vocative case of nouns (marked by a penultimate accent), as well as in the Indirect Evidential (which he terms "Indirective Evidential") verb forms (marked by an initial accent).

Although Hsieh's analysis is able to account for most of

the surface tonal patterns he observed, some analytical inconsistencies exist in the system he proposes. For one, Hsieh claims that the tonal contrast between /H/ and /HL/ is restricted to underived and non-inflected words. However, later in the same study, he documents examples of what he terms "High-toned" patterns on an array of deverbal nouns (see (3)), which, of course, are not underived.

(3) Deverbal nouns (Hsieh 1999: 160)

Verb Stem		Gloss	Deverbal Noun		Gloss
-pkôr2^2	[HL]	'carry on back'	sa-pkór	[L-H]	'belt for carrying on back'
-mpʰə̂r	[HL]	'sell'	sa-mpʰúr	[L-H]	'marketplace'
prêt	[HL]	'break'	sa-prát	[L-H]	'breaking tool'

The other inconsistency occurs when High-toned words of four or more syllables are examined. For example, in introducing his word tone system, Hsieh analyzes the quadrisyllabic word kʰarʝalili [L-H-H-L] 'swallow (bird)' as a High-toned word which gets a Low on the final syllable because words of four

---

2   The tonal notations employed in Hsieh 1999 are:

σ̂	/HL/	(Falling tone)
σ́	/H/	(High tone)

syllables or longer cannot have a High tone at the end of a prosodic word. Nonetheless, the same word (i.e., *kʰarʲalili* [L-H-H-L] 'swallow (bird)') is also characterized as a prosodic word carrying penultimate accent (as already shown above in (2)). Such inconsistencies suggest that 1) with respect to tonal behaviors, the distinction between lexicon and grammar is not easy to maintain and 2) treating tone and pitch-accent as two parallel systems for Cogtse can be problematic, as these two systems seem to interact with each other.

Y. Lin (2002; 2003) avoids the above-mentioned problems by proposing an analysis in which pitch-accent interplays with tone on both lexical and grammatical levels. In this hybrid system, pitch-accent is realized "by a high pitch on the accented syllable followed by a low pitch in the following syllable" (Cruttenden 1997: 10). Pitch shapes of unaccented syllables in Cogtse are predictable. That is, except for the unaccented initial syllable, which is always on a low pitch, unaccented syllables leading to the accent are spoken on a high pitch, and post-accent syllables are automatically on a low pitch. In addition to pitch-accent, Cogtse exhibits two contrastive tones-- (High) Level and Falling-- on the accented final syllable. In other words, non-final accent is realized with a Level tone, but a final accent can be associated to either a Level or Falling, which is lexically determined. The trisyllabic examples in (4a-b) below are both accented on the final syllable underlyingly.

They show a contrast between Level and Falling tones, and the surface shape of the words is predictable.

(4) a. 'flail' b. 'shoulder pole'

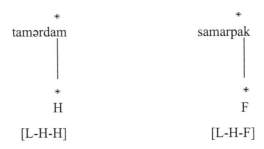

Y. Lin suggests that the interactions between pitch-accent and tone permeate all the lexical and grammatical tonal patterns in Cogtse. There is a phonologically-conditioned accent shift that occurs when the final level tone is on a prosodic word of four or more syllables. The shift replaces the final level tone with a penultimate accent, whereas words with the falling tone remain unaffected. Contrast (5) and (6), which exemplify quadri-syllabic words formed via derivational prefixation to disyllabic words under level and falling tones. Note that when they become quadrisyllabic or longer, the final level tone is replaced by penultimate accent (5c), and the final falling tone stays invariant (6b-c).

(5)

a.

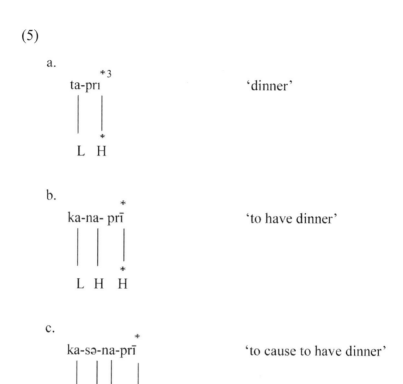

ta-prı   *3   'dinner'

L   H

b.

ka-na- prī   'to have dinner'

L   H   H

c.

ka-sə-na-prī   'to cause to have dinner'

L   H   H   H

---

3   The tone and accentual markings applied in Y. Lin (2003) are:

    σ̂   Syllable on Falling tone   σ̄   Syllable on Level tone

    σ́   Accented syllable

(6)

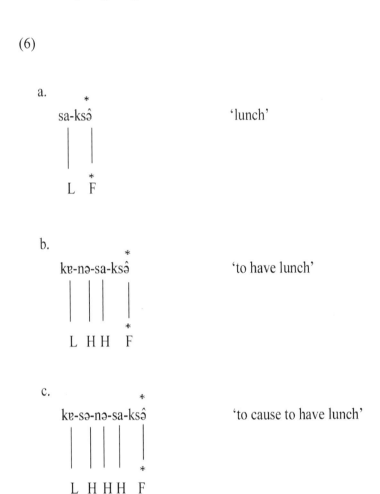

Y. Lin (2000; 2003) discovers that tone and pitch-accent play a crucial role in Cogtse grammar. This is a major breakthrough within the study of Cogtse word prosody. Based on this discovery, it is confirmed that Cogtse is by no means atonal, nor are tonal modifications merely restricted to a limited range of uses. Instead, tones are employed to contrast lexical meanings; and meanwhile they also serve as an indispensable device for the formation of all sorts of grammatical categories. For instance, Indirect Evidential verbs must take an initial accent; Vocative nouns and Observational verbs are uniformly accented on the penultimate syllable; and the tonal patterns of a compound are determined by the tonal value of the second component. In particular, the verb Stem1-Stem2 alternation[4] requires tonal and accentual modifications that preserve the two-way tonal contrast. Namely, in Stem1 forms an input falling tone remains falling, while level tone is replaced by penultimate accent; and in Stem2 forms, an input falling tone is replaced by penultimate accent, and level tone shifts to falling.

While an approach integrating pitch-accent and tone can hold up against the tonal phenomena in Cogtse, controversies have been surrounding the analytical adequacy and typological position of the notion of "pitch-accent". The following section (§2.2) considers these controversies.

---

4   Based on a detailed study of stem alternation in Showu (another Rgyalrong language) and comparative evidence across three Rgyalrong dialects (Showu, Tshobdun, and Japhug), J. Sun (2004) reports a three-way stem alternation for the Rgyalrongic verb: Stem3 (of transitive, non-past/ non-progressive, non-SAP singular arguments); Stem2 (required in perfective and past imperfective as well as the (primary) progressive); Stem1 (elsewhere).

2.2. Typological and Analytical Problems with Pitch-Accent

As Yip states, pitch-accent is a convenient term for a special kind of language that uses tone in a rather limited way. In such languages, one or two tone melodies are either lexically associated to specific Tone-Bearing Units (TBUs) or are attracted to a syllable that is rhythmically prominent (Yip 2002: 260). Therefore, for instance, for the majority of Japanese dialects, there is no need to specify the pitch of each individual syllable. With diacritic markers and a set of rules, the pitch shape of the whole phrase can be predicted (Shibatani 1990: 177). Even for languages that do not lexically distinguish "accented" and "unaccented" words, tonal rules can sometimes be usefully formulated in accentual terms. For example, Somali nouns only have a High tone whose distinctiveness resides in its location (i.e., on the last or penultimate mora) (Gussenhoven 2004: 39). In short, "considerations of functional explanation have weighed in favor of accent" (Odden 1999: 189).

Meanwhile, however, the notion of "pitch-accent" has given rise to various concerns about its typological status and analytical adequacy. A number of linguists have argued against the pitch-accent approach due to considerations of theoretical simplicity (Odden 1999: 189). Within the field of phonological typology, Hyman (2006; 2007) argues that "pitch-accent" does not constitute a phonological prototype because it is not a coherent notion that stands independent of the two highest-level typological prototypes-- tone and stress (Hyman 2006: 236). He observes that by "pitch-accent" linguists have generally been referring to one or more of the following properties: 1) a system whose underlying prosody and surface realizations are different; 2) a system in which tone and stress interact; 3) a system in which tone is restricted, sparse or privative (Hyman 2006: 236-237). Culminativity (i.e., every word has at most one accent) is often referred to as a diagnostic characteristic to distinguish pitch-accent from tone. However, as Hyman (2006: 238-239) notes, culminativity does not have to be restricted to tonal features, so it is not a sufficient characteristic to define "pitch-accent" as a distinct type. A language can have culminative glottalized consonants, for example. but this does not make the language a "glottal accent language" in prosodic typology. In fact, Hyman suggests that languages identified as having a pitch-accent system in fact freely "pick and choose" between the prototypical features of stress-accent and tone; and such intermediate word-prosodic systems should not be considered as discrete types (2006: 226). In particular, Hyman points out that languages that have sparsely distributed tones (such as one High tone per word) have also been analyzed as having a "restricted tone system" (Hyman 2006; Schadeberg 1973; Voorhoeve 1973).

Instead of referring to pitch-accent as one of the highest-level typological prototypes, various linguists propose pitch-accent to be a subtype of tone. Donohue (1997), for example, suggests that the prototype "tone" can be broken down into three primary subtypes: syllable-tone, word-tone, and pitch-accent. However, despite this, the analytical problems of the pitch-accent approach still remain. At least three aspects of analytical inadequacy have been pointed out. The first considers the origin and essence of the notion "pitch-accent" and diacritics ("*" in most cases). Beckman (1986) introduced the term "stress accent" to refer to a situation in which syllabic prominence is signaled by F0 as well as duration and other features. The term is then used to contrast with "pitch-accent", where prominence is signaled by F0 alone. "Accent" therefore becomes equivalent to "phonological prominence" (Gussenhoven 2004: 47). In a stress language, prominence relations are formally represent-ted as metrical trees or grids. In cases where foot construc-tion is not completely predictable by general rules, diacritics are introduced for one specific purpose: to trigger the formation of feet. However, in a pitch-accent language like Japanese (which shows the first and the third "pitch-accent" properties summarized by Hyman above), the diacritics do not induce the creation of any metrical structure, but just determine the assignment of tones (Pulleyblank 1986: 156). In other words, in such languages, "accent" is used only to indicate pitch, and nothing "accentual is to be observed in the system.

The second analytical problem with pitch-accent is that the diacritics are a much more powerful device than a strictly tonal or strictly stress analysis. Specifically, a pitch-accent approach allows for many rule types, including accentual rules, tone rules, as well as rules related to tone and accentual diacritics. Given the commonly accepted phonological strategy that a theory should be as restrictive as possible, an alternative approach should be chosen over such an exceedingly powerful approach as pitch-accent unless it is impossible to do so.

The analytical inadequacy of employing "pitch-accent" can also be seen in the tonal association to diacritics for tone melody assignment. In an analysis in which accent is signaled by a pitch drop, for example, a sequence of tones (i.e., H L) is assigned to an accented unit.

(7) (adapted from Pulleyblank 1986: 162)

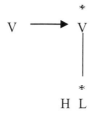

In such a case, the two tones are fully realized if there is enough space for one-to-one mapping between tones and TBUs. If there is only one TBU, the sequence of tones crowds, and TBU surfaces as a falling contour [HL].

However, as Pulleyblank (1986: 162) argues, once it is accepted that sequences of tones can be assigned to a single element, then it becomes possible to posit all sorts of rules that allow the assignment of sequences of phonological features to a single element. For instance, there could be rules that insert "harmony melodies":

(8) (Pulleyblank 1986: 162)

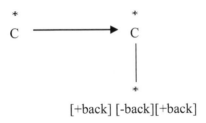

[+back] [-back][+back]

Allowing for such rules would considerably vitiate the analytical power of phonological theory, unless stringent constraints are imposed on the kinds of sequence that can make up "prosodic melodies" in a legitimate way (Pulleyblank 1986: 162).

In sum, the above arguments against the notion of "pitch-accent" converge on the conclusion that, although the "tone and pitch-accent" approach works well for Cogtse, it weakens phonological theory substantially, whether in terms of typology or analytical methodology. A more satisfactory analysis of Cogtse word prosody is thus in order. Therefore, the following section will show that it is indeed possible to analyze Cogtse word prosody in strictly tonal terms.

2.3. A Privative Interpretation of Cogtse Tone[5]

In Cogtse, tones serve to mark semantic, lexical and grammatical distinctions. Cogtse lacks a length or syllable weight distinction, so each syllable is one mora. The tonebearing unit in Cogtse, therefore. is the syllable or mora. The attested surface tonal sequences in the Cogtse word are as follows. The patterns in (9a) and (9b) are realizations of Surface-Melody 1, as will be examined in §2.3.1. Patterns in (9c) are realizations of Surface-Melody 2, and will be discussed in §2.3.2. The surface patterns in (9d) are observed in the Indirect Evidential verb form.

---

5 I would like to thank Jonathan Evans for all the kind help and useful suggestions that were generously provided while I was shaping the content of this analysis. All remaining errors are mine.

(9) Cogtse tonal patterns

H: High Level   F: Falling   L: Low Level

	1-syllable	2-syllable	3-syllable	4-syllable	5-syllable
a.	H	L-H	L-H-H	L-H-H-L	L-H-H-H-L
b.	HL	L-HL	L-H-HL	L-H-H-HL	L-H-H-H-HL
c.	L	H-L	L-H-L	L-H-H-L	L-H-H-H-L
d.			H-H-L	H-H-L-L	H-H-L-L-L
e.			H-L-L	H-L-L-L	H-L-L-L-L

The surface restrictions of the tonal patterns are summarized below.

(10) Surface restrictions observed for the tonal patterns

    a. Monosyllabic words can occur with H, L, or HL
    b. HL only occurs on the rightmost edge
    c. H can occur at initial, medial, and final positions
    d. On prosodic words of four or more syllables, H never occurs on the rightmost edge
    e. L only occurs on the edge, but a sequence of Ls on the rightmost edge is allowed (as in 9d-e)
    f. There is no sequence *H-L-H or *H-L-L-H; that is, a word does not have more than one peak.

In this study, I present the falling tone as /HL/. I will argue that word prosody in Cogtse is an underlyingly privative system in which /HL/ contrasts with /Ø/ (zero), with /HL/ being the more restricted (hence marked) tone, and toneless (/Ø/) words surface with fixed and predictable tonal patterns. While falling-toned words surface with one single pattern everywhere,[6] toneless words surface with either of two melodies (which I term Surface-Melody 1 and Surface-Melody 2) depending on the contexts in which they occur. The difference, however, can be accounted for by changing the ordering of the tonal rules that involve foot types and the direction of foot parsing, as will be demonstrated in §2.3.1 and §2.3.2 In the subsequent section, we start by examining Surface-Melody 1.

2.3.1. Surface-Melody 1

In (11), examples of Surface-Melody 1 on words of one to four syllables are provided. These surface patterns, also shown in (9a) and (9b), are observed on Cogtse nouns (including deverbal nouns) and nominalized verbs in the citation form.

6　The Indirect Evidential verb constitutes an exception. It is assigned /HL/ on the initial instead of the final syllable, and is thus realized on a special melody.

(11) Cogtse Surface-Melody 1 and examples

	Monosyllabic	Disyllabic	Trisyllabic	Quadrisyllabic
a.	**H**	**L-H**	**L-H-H**	**L-H-H-L**
	(Nouns)			
	ʒo	kə-jo	ta-me-ndzo	a-bu-ru-ru
	'curd'	'sheep'	'toe'	'snail'

	(Verbs in citation)			
	---[7]	ka-za	ka-ntʃi-rət	kɐ-nɐ-ŋkʰsəŋkʰsət
		'to eat'	'to squeeze'	'to smell'
	(Deverbal nominalized nouns)			
	---[8]	sa-za	sa-ntʃi-rət	sɐ-nɐ-ŋkʰsəŋkʰsət
		'dining place/tool'	'squeezing tool'	'smelling tool'

b.	**HL**	**L-HL**	**L-H-HL**	**L-H-H-HL**
	(Nouns)			
	ca	kʰa-ʃpa	tə-po-prɐm	ŋgo-mpo-kʰa-ʃna
	'musk deer'	'frog'	'large intestine'	'(a kind of) spider'
	(Verbs in citation)			
	---	kɐ-mpʰər	ka-nə-na	ka-nə-mcɐ-rɐ
		'to wrap'	'to rest'	'to watch, to read'

---

7 Verbs in the citation form are prefixed with the nominalizers *ka-* or *kə-*, so they must have at least two syllables. For detailed discussion of the distinction between *ka-* and *kə-*, see Sun (2007b), and Sun and Lin (2007).

8 Deverbal nouns are formed with an oblique nominalizer *sa-~sɐ-* plus verb stem, and are thus minimally disyllabic.

(Deverbal nominalized nouns)

---	sɐ-mpʰər	sa-nə-na	sa-nə-mcɐ-rɐ
	'wraping place/tool'	'resting place'	'reading place/tool'

Notice that the number of tonal sequences does not increase with the number of syllables. In fact, surface patterns as such prompted Hsieh (1999) to propose for Cogtse a "word-tone" analysis in which /H/ contrasts with /HL/. According to Hsieh (1999: 109-110), one only has to specify /H/ (Tone 1) or /HL/ (Tone 2) for each word in the underlying representation, then surface restrictions will "filter out" the expected surface tonal patterns.[9]

In fact, disyllabic minimal pairs such as those shown below in (12) do make it tempting to assume that the underlying tonal contrast is between /H/ and /HL/.

---

9 Recall that, as summarized in §0, the "word tone" system is proposed to account for what Hsieh (1999) terms "lexical tonal patterns". For the phrasal and grammatical levels, pitch-accent is introduced.

(12) Disyllabic minimal pairs contrasting in tone

	[L-H]		[L-HL]	
a.	ka-po	'to spin yarn (NMZL)'	ka-po	'to come; to bake (NMZL)
b.	tə-po	'moxa'	tə-po	'intestines'
c.	ka-rma	'to sleep (NMZL)'	ka-rma	'Tibetan eared pheasant'
d.	kə-jo	'sheep'	kə-jo	'to be light (NMZL)'
e.	ta-ro	'leader'	ta-ro	'chest (body part)'
f.	kə-tʃor	'to be narrow (NMZL)'	kə-tʃor	'to be sour'
g.	kə-jam	'sun'	kə-jam	'to be spacious'
h.	kə-lok	'white conch'	kə-lok	'shepherd'

In the present analysis, however, I will show that Cogtse word prosody, taking the whole word as the domain of tonal contrast, distinguishes /HL/ from /Ø/. In other words, underlyingly, only /HL/ has to be specified. Unless required by the grammar (i.e., the Indirect Evidential assigns /HL/ to the initial syllable of a verb), /HL/ is prelinked to the final syllable of a word. A word can be either toneless, or specified with /HL/, and the surface melody is derivable using a set of tone rules that specify foot parsing, foot types, tone spreading and association.

Taking trisyllabic patterns for example, three rules are required to derive the surface melodies for falling-toned words and the toneless nouns and verbs in the citation form. It is assumed that every Cogtse word is parsed from both edges by an iambic foot (Left) and a trochaic foot (Right). In addition, this language allows non-initial degenerate feet. Each foot head is then associated to Hs. Finally, Ls are inserted on toneless syllables.

(13) **Ft Parsing (L, iambic):** Parse a word from the left edge by a binary, iambic foot

(14) **Ft Parsing (R, trochaic):** Parse a word from the right edge by a binary, trochaic foot

(15) **Degenerate Ft:** A remaining free single syllable forms monosyllabic foot if it is not word-initial.

(16) **Obligatory H:** Each foot head is associated to a H

(17) **Default L:** Insert L onto toneless syllables

To derive Surface-Melody 1, the rule of iambic footing is applied prior to the rule of trochaic footing. The rules should thus be applied in the following order:

(18) Rule Ordering in Melody 1

Ft Parsing (L, iambic) (13) > Ft Parsing (R, trochaic) (14) > Degenerate Ft (15) > Obligatory H (16) > Default L (17)

Consider the derivations in (19).

(19)

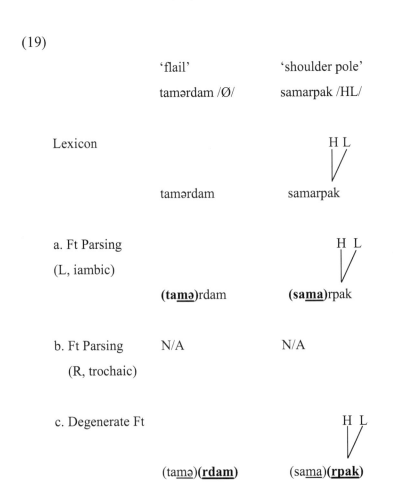

	'flail'	'shoulder pole'
	tamərdam /Ø/	samarpak /HL/
Lexicon		H L
	tamərdam	samarpak
a. Ft Parsing (L, iambic)		H L
	(tamə)rdam	**(sama)**rpak
b. Ft Parsing (R, trochaic)	N/A	N/A
c. Degenerate Ft		H L
	(tamə)**(rdam)**	(sama)**(rpak)**

d. Obligatory H

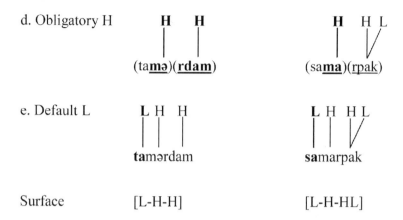

e. Default L

Surface   [L-H-H]   [L-H-HL]

Words of four or more syllables show an important tonal property that H never occurs on the rightmost edge. I assume this is because quadrisyllabic or longer words provide enough space to manifest the effect of both foot-parsing rules (13)-(14). Similar coexisting and completing stress rules are also observed in Stoney Dakota. The language assigns two stresses on a prosodic word, one on the initial or second syllable, and the other on the penultimate or final syllable. Only on words of four or more syllables can the stress rules fully apply (Shaw 1985: 14-15).[10]

Consider the derivation of the Cogtse verbs 'to cause to have dinner' (/Ø/) and 'to have lunch' (/HL/).

---

10 I am grateful to Matthew Gordon for bringing this work to my attention.

(20)

	'to cause to have dinner'	'to have lunch'
	kasənapri /Ø/	kɐnəsaksə/HL/

Lexicon

| | kasənapri | kɐnəsaksə |

a. Ft Parsing
(L, iambic)

| | **(kasə)**napri | **(kɐnə)**saksə |

b. Ft Parsing
   (R,
trochaic)

| | (kasə)**(napri)** | (kɐnə)**(saksə)** |

c. Degenerate   N/A   N/A
Ft

d. Obligatory
H

| | (kasə)(**na**pri) | (kɐnə)(**sa**ksə) |

e. Default L

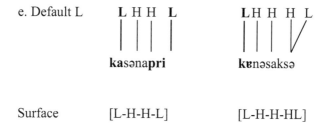

| Surface | [L-H-H-L] | [L-H-H-HL] |

The other tonal property observed is that Hs occur sequentially. There is no such sequence as *H-L-H. For example, the pentasyllabic word *kɐsənəsaksə̂* 'to cause to have lunch' surfaces as [L-H-H-H-HL]. I assume that Hs are inserted to toneless syllables between two Hs to achieve a plateau-like H-sequence in the case at hand.

(21) **H-Insertion**: Insert an H to toneless syllables between two Hs

The rule should be applied after Obligatory H (16):

(22) Rule Ordering in Melody 1
Ft Parsing (L, iambic) (13) > Ft Parsing (R, trochaic) (14) > Degenerate Ft (15) > Obligatory H (16) > **H-Insertion (21)** > Default L (17)

See the derivation of the sexisyllabic word in (23):

(23)

'to cause (some people) to shout to each other'

kɐsəŋɐnɐkʰokʰo /HL/

Lexicon

H L

kɐsəŋɐnɐkʰokʰo

a. Ft Parsing
(L, iambic)

H L

(kɐ<u>sə</u>)ŋɐnɐkʰokʰo

b. Ft Parsing
  (R, trochaic)

H L

(kɐ<u>sə</u>)ŋɐnɐ(**kʰokʰo**)

c. Degenerate
Ft

N/A

d. Obligatory H

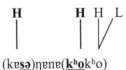

(kɐ<u>sə</u>)ŋɐnɐ(**kʰok**ʰo)

e. H-Insertion

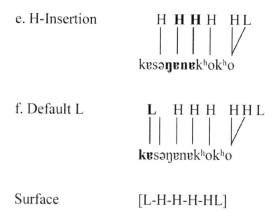

H **H H** H H L

kɐsəŋɐnɐkʰokʰo

f. Default L

L H H H H H L

kɐsəŋɐnɐkʰokʰo

Surface   [L-H-H-H-HL]

It has been shown in this section that Cogtse word prosody has an underlying system of /HL, Ø/. Underlyingly, only /HL/ has to be specified, then the surface melody can be realized by the application of a set of tone rules. Surface-Melody 1 parses a word from the left before parsing the same word from the right. In transcribing tones, I will leave toneless words unmarked, and mark /HL/ with a circumflex on the falling-toned syllable. For example:

(24)

/Ø/	pak	'pig'	[H]
	tə-po	'moxa'	[L-H]
	ka-ŋa-kru	'to cry'	[L-H-H]
	kʰa-rʝa-li-li	'swallow (bird)'	[L-H-H-L]

/HL/	ʃâ	'flesh, muscle'	[HL]
	tə-pô	'intestines'	[L-HL]
	ka-nə-wô	'to be sick'	[L-H-HL]
	kɐ-sɐ-co-lô	'to mix'	[L-H-H-HL]

2.3.2. Surface-Melody 2

There exists one other surface melody for toneless words in Cogtse. The melody is observed on verbs, nouns in the vocative case, and ideophones. Note that this second surface melody is only observed on toneless words and falling-toned words in the same contexts still surface with Melody 1. One thing that is crucial is that these two different surface melodies are in complementary distribution. In other words, for example, one would never see a perfective verb occur with both Melody 1 and Melody 2.

Below are the attested surface patterns of /Ø/ and /HL/ on verbs and vocative nouns. The surface melody of /Ø/ is different from its Melody-1 counterpart, while the melody of /HL/ remains invariant in all contexts (i.e., contexts in which toneless words have to switch between Surface-Melody 1 and Surface-Melody 2.)

(25) Surface melody of verbs and vocative nouns

	Monosyllabic	Disyllabic	Trisyllabic	Quadrisyllabic
/Ø/	**L**	**H-L**	**L-H-L**	**L-H-H-L**
(Verbs)				
	rjap	nə-ɲir	to-wa-tsor	to-nə-sa-ksə
	'(s/he) will stand'	'(s/he)	'(it)	'(s/he) had lunch'
	(Non-Past)[11]	changed'	cracked'	(Perfective)
		(Perfective)	(Perfective)	
(Vocative nouns)				
	---[12]	kra-ʃes	kra-ʃi-smon	mtsʰo-mo-scit
		'Krashis (PN)'	'Krashismon	'Tshomoscit (PN)'
			(PN)'	
(Ideophones)				
	---	boj-boj[13]	---	---
		'choppy, fleshy'		

---

11 The Perfective is formed with one of the seven orientationally specified perfective prefixes (*to-* 'upward', *na-* 'downward', *ko-* 'eastwards', *nə-* 'westwards', *ro-* 'upstream', *rə-* 'downstream', *ja-* (orientationally neutral) and verb stem. Non-past forms are bare verb stems.

12 Cogtse person names are disyllabic at a minimum.

13 Unlike ideophones in the Caodeng dialect of Rgyalrong, which can be of one to four syllables , ideophones in Cogtse are almost always disyllabic. Cf. for argumentation of ideophones as a distinct lexical category in Caodeng Rgyalrong.

/HL/	HL	L-HL	L-H-HL	L-H-H-HL

(Verbs)

	nɟîr	to-rjâp	to-nə-pjôl	to-nɐ-ŋkʰsər-ŋkʰsə̂r
	'(s/he) will change'	'(s/he) stood'	'(s/he)	'(s/he) smelt'
	(Non-Past)	(Perfective)	detoured'	(Perfective)
			(Perfective)	

(Vocative nouns)

	---	kra-ʃes	kra-ʃi-smon	mtsʰo-mo-scit
		'Krashis (PN)'	'Krashismon	'Tshomoscit (PN)'
			(PN)'	

In these contexts of Surface-Melody 2, the contrast between /HL/ and /Ø/ is still maintained. Grammatical differences can be expressed by changes of the tonal values over the same segments. For example, the following verb forms of 'stand' differ only in tone, but respectively denote perfective and imperative meanings.

(26) Perfective and imperative contrasting by tone

Grammatical Category	Verb Form	Tone	Surface Form	Gloss
Imperative:	to-rjap IMP-stand$_1$	/Ø/	[H-L]	'Stand up!'
Perfective:	to-rjâp PV-stand$_2$	/HL/	[L-HL]	'S/he stood up'

Now, compare the two sets of toneless patterns in (27):

(27) /Ø/-1= Melody 1   /Ø/-2= Melody 2

	Monosyllabic	Disyllabic	Trisyllabic	Quadrisyllabic
/Ø/-1	H	L-H	L-H-H	L-H-H-L
/Ø/-2	L	H-L	L-H-L	L-H-H-L

The /Ø/-2 Melody is different from the /Ø/-1 melody in the following aspects. Note that the differences are only observed on words of three or fewer syllables. Quadrisyllabic or longer words surface with the same pattern in all contexts.

(28)

    a. Monosyllabic toneless words surface as L instead of H

    b. Disyllabic words surface as H-L instead of L-H

    c. Trisyllabic words surface as L-H-L instead of L-H-H

    d. No H is allowed word finally, even in words of three or fewer syllables.

I assume that the differences result from a switch in the ordering of the two parsing rules. While Melody 1 starts the foot-parsing processes from the left, Melody 2 starts parsing a word from the right. All the related tonal rules are applied in the order as represented below in (29) to derive Melody 2.

Compare it with the rule ordering of Melody 1 in (22). The differences lie on the two foot-parsing rules ((13) and (14)).

(29) Rule ordering of Melody 2

Ft Parsing (R, trochaic) (14) > Ft Parsing (L, iambic) (13) >

Degenerate Ft (15) > Obligatory H (16) > H-Insertion (21) > Default L (17)

The derivation processes in (30) illustrate how the Imperative verb form of 'stand' (monosyllabic), the ideophone 'chubby, fleshy' (disyllabic), and the Perfective form of 'crack' (trisyllabic) achieve their surface realizations.

(30)

	'(s/he) stands' (Non-Past)	'chubby, fleshy, very cute, with rosy complexion' (Ideophone)	'(it) cracked' (Perfective)
	rjap /Ø/	bojboj /Ø/	towatsor /Ø/
Lexicon	rjap	bojboj	towatsor
a. Ft Parsing (R, trochaic)	N/A	(**bojboj**)	to(**watsor**)

b. Ft Parsing (L, iambic)	N/A	N/A	N/A
c. Degenerate Ft	**rjap**	N/A	**to**(<u>wat</u>sor)
d. Obligatory H	N/A	H | (**bo**jboj)	H | to(<u>wat</u>sor)
e. H-Insertion	N/A	N/A	N/A
f. Default L	L | **rjap**	H L | | boj**boj**	L H L | | | **to**wat**sor**
Surface	[L]	[H-L]	[L-H-L]

Words of four or more syllables surface with the same surface pattern in the contexts for both Melody 1 and Melody 2 (see the surface patterns of quadrisyllabic /Ø/ and /HL/ in (20)). Below in (31) are two Perfective verbs (respectively quadrisyllabic and pentasyllabic). Although they are in Melody 2 contexts, and are derived using the tonal rules and rule ordering proposed for Melody 2 (as shown in (29)), these two words surface with the same tonal patterns as quadrisyllabic and longer words do in Melody-1 contexts.

(31) Quadrisyllabic Perfective verb

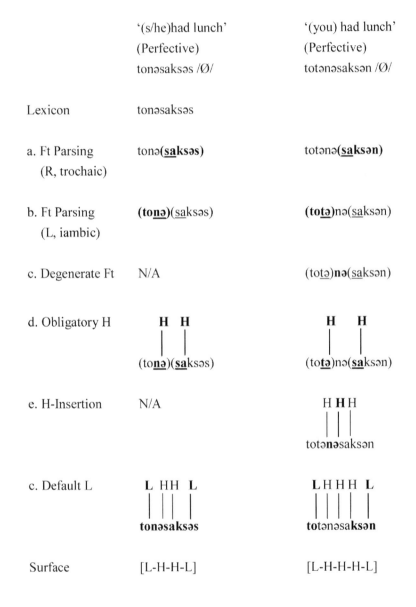

	'(s/he)had lunch' (Perfective) tonəsaksəs /Ø/	'(you) had lunch' (Perfective) totənəsaksən /Ø/
Lexicon	tonəsaksəs	
a. Ft Parsing (R, trochaic)	tonə(**saksəs**)	totənə(**saksən**)
b. Ft Parsing (L, iambic)	(to**nə**)(saksəs)	(to**tə**)nə(saksən)
c. Degenerate Ft	N/A	(to**tə**)**nə**(saksən)
d. Obligatory H	H H | | (to**nə**)(**sak**səs)	H H | | (to**tə**)nə(**sak**sən)
e. H-Insertion	N/A	H **H** H | | | totənəsaksən
c. Default L	L HH L |||| **tonəsaksəs**	L H H H L ||||| **totənəsaksən**
Surface	[L-H-H-L]	[L-H-H-H-L]

I have introduced rules by which the underlying contrastive /HL/ and /Ø/ achieve their surface realizations. The surface variations of /Ø/ turn out to be context-sensitive. That is, toneless words surface with different melodies depending on the grammatical contexts they occur.

Table 2.1 summarizes the distribution of the two surface melodies of toneless words in Cogtse. Notice again that falling-toned words always stick to Melody 1.

	Melody 1	Melody 2
Nouns	All but in vocative case	Vocative case
Verbs	Citation form (nominalized with *ka-* or *kə-*)	Inflected verbs

Table 2.1 Distribution of Melody 1 and Melody 2 of toneless words

In the following section (§2.3.3), I will demonstrate how tone is applied to denote different grammatical meanings.

2 3 3.Grammatical Tonal Variations

Tone in Cogtse not only functions to contrast lexical meanings but is of great importance to the grammar of the language. In terms of tonal behaviors, the tonal modifications involved in grammar can be classified into three types. In the first type, grammatical alternations preserve the two-way tonal contrast between /HL/ and /Ø/ (§2.3.3.1). In the second type, the tone of one of the constituent morphemes is retained

(§2.3.3.2). In the third type, morphosyntactic environments assign a definite tone irrespective of the inherent tone of the constituent morphemes (§2.3.3.3).

2.3.3.1. Tonal Modification Preserving the Two-Way Contrast

Two grammatical processes--Stem1-Stem2 alternation (§2.3.3.1) and nominal plural and dual cliticization (§2.3.3.1.2)-- preserve, though in different ways, the binary tonal contrast between /HL/ and /Ø/.

2.3.3.1.1. Stem1-Stem2 Alternation

Cogtse verbs have two stems that are employed in different grammatical constructions. Stem1 forms include other-person Present Imperfective [*ŋɐ-(~ŋɐ-)* + Stem1], Non-Past (unprefixed Stem1), Imperative [PV + Stem1], and Irrealis [IRR + PV/IMPFV + Stem1]. Stem2 forms are Perfective [PV + Stem2], Past Imperfective [*na-(~nɐ-)* + Stem2], and self-person Present Imperfective [*ko-* + Stem2]. While only twenty percent of Cogtse verbs distinguish two verb stems via ablaut, almost all verbs resort to tone to achieve stem alternation. This morphological process involves tone polarity. That is, if a verb has /HL/ in its Stem1 form, then it switches to /Ø/ to achieve its Stem2 form; and if a verb is toneless (/Ø/) in its Stem1 form, then its Stem2 form is falling-toned (/HL/).

(32) Stem1-Stem2 alternation: Flip-flop between /HL/ and /Ø/

(Alternation 1)

| **Stem1** | L | H-L | L-H-H-L | L-H-L | /Ø/ |
| **Stem2** | HL | L-HL | L-H-H-HL | L-H-HL | /HL/ |

(Alternation 2)

| **Stem1** | HL | L-HL | L-H-H-HL | L-H-HL | /HL/ |
| **Stem2** | L | H-L | L-H-H-L | L-H-L | /Ø/ |

Following are examples of the above-mentioned gram-matical constructions showing Stem1-Stem2 alternation for two verbs of inherently distinctive tones: 'to dig' and 'to stand'. Examples in (33) and (34) show a flip-flop from /HL/ to /Ø/ for Stem1-Stem2 alternation of 'to dig' (The variations are summarized above in Alternation 2)

(33) 'to dig' STEM1 (/HL/)

    a. Other-person Present Imperfective

       wəjo   **ŋa-lwâ-w (L-HL)**   **[ŋà-lwâw]**[14]

       3SG   IMPFV-dig$_1$-TR

       'He is digging'

---

14 In the phonetic transcription within square brackets, the grave accent (σ̀) represents L tone, the acute accent (σ́) represents H tone, and the circumflex (σ̂) represents Falling tone.

b. Non-Past

ŋa	stoŋsni	lwâ-ŋ (HL)	[lwâŋ]
1SG	every.day	dig$_1$:NPST-1SG	

'I dig every day'

c. Imperative

na-lwâ-w (L-HL)   [nà-lwâw]

IMP-dig$_1$-TR

'(You sg.) dig!'

d. Irrealis used as a Jussive

wəjo=kə	a-to-lwâ-w (L-H-HL)	[à-tó-lwâw]
3SG=ERG	IRR-PV-dig$_1$-TR	

'Let him dig!'

(34) 'to dig' STEM2 (/Ø/)

a. Perfective

wəjo	to-lwa-w (H-L)	[tó-lwàw]
3SG	PV-dig$_2$-TR	

'He dug'

b. Past Imperfective

wəjo	na-lwa-w (H-L)	[ná-lwàw]
3SG	IMPFV:PST-dig$_2$-TR	

'He was digging'

c. Self-person Present Imperfective

ŋa   **ko-lwa-ŋ (H-L)**   **[kó-lwàŋ]**

1SG   IMPFV-dig$_2$-1SG

'I am digging'

Examples in (35) and (36) show a flip-flop from /Ø/ to /HL/ for Stem1-Stem2 alternation of 'to stand':

(35) 'to stand' STEM1 /Ø/

    a. Other-person Present Imperfective

       wəjo   **ŋa-rjap (H-L)**   **[ŋá-rjàp]**

       3SG   IMPFV-stand$_1$

       'He is standing'

    b. Non-Past

       ŋa   stoŋsni   **rjap-ŋ (L)**   **[rjàm]**

       1SG   every.day   stand$_1$:NPST-1SG

       'I stand every day'

    c. Imperative

       to-rjap (H-L)   **[tó-rjàp]**

       IMP-stand$_1$

       '(You sg.) stand up!'

    d. Irrealis used as a Jussive

wəjo **a-to-rjap (L-H-L)** **[à-tó-rjàp]**

3SG IRR-PV-stand₁

'Let him stand!'

(36) 'to stand' STEM2 /HL/

a. Perfective

wəjo **to-rjâp (L-HL)** **[tò-rjâp]**

3SG PV-stand₂

b. Past Imperfective

wəjo **na-rjap (L-HL)** **[nà-rjâp]**

1SG IMPFV:PST-stand₂

c. Self-person Present Imperfective

ŋa **ko-rjâp-ŋ (L-HL)** **[kò-rjâm]**

1SG IMPFV-stand₂-1SG

2.3.3.1.2. Toned Clitics: Dual and Plural Cliticization

Nominal dual and plural markers are enclitics with the noun phrase being their domain.

(37)

pak	'pig'
pak=ɲê	'pigs'
pak kə-tsʰo	'big pig' [pig NMZL-be.big]
pak kə-tsʰo=ɲê	'big pigs'

Two tonal patterns are observed in nominal plural and dual forms, and the differences seem to derive from an interaction of the inherent tone of the enclitics and their hosts. Compare the patterns on the examples in (38) and (39):

(38)Pattern 1

	Singular (/Ø/)	**Dual**	**Plural**	**Gloss**
a.	pak	pak=ndʒes	pak=ɲe	'pig'
	[H]	[L-HL]	[L-HL]	
b.	toru	toru=ndʒes	toru=ɲe	'cat'
	[L-H]	[L-H-HL]	[L-H-HL]	
c.	kʰɐmtsərɟok	kʰɐmtsərɟok=ndʒes	kʰɐmtsərɟok=ɲe	'lizard'
	[L-H-H]	[L-H-H-HL]	[L-H-H-HL]	

(39)Pattern 2

Singular (/HL/)	Dual	Plural	Gloss
a. ca	ca=ndʒes	ca=ɲe	'pig'
[HL]	[H-L]	[H-L]	
b. rdəgə	rdəgə=ndʒes	rdəgə=ɲe	'argali'
[L-HL]	[L-H-L]	[L-H-L]	
c. laŋpotʃʰe	laŋpotʃʰe=ndʒes	laŋpotʃʰe=ɲe	'elephant
[L-H-HL]	[L-H-H-L]	[L-H-H-L]	

Note that in Pattern 1 (38), the dual and plural forms of toneless stems all end with a falling-toned syllable, which happens to be the plural or dual marker. However, in Pattern 2 (39), all the plural and dual markers are on L. To account for the variations, I assume that the dual and plural enclitics have an inherent /HL/:

(40)

When the host of the enclitics is toneless (like the examples in (38)), the whole cliticized form surfaces as /HL/:

(41)   'pigs (PL)': pak + =ɲê

$$
\begin{array}{ccccc}
\text{H L} & & \text{H L} & \text{L H L} & \\
\vee & & \vee & |\ \vee & \\
\text{pak} \quad +\text{ɲe} & \rightarrow \text{pakɲe} & \rightarrow \text{pakɲe} & & \text{[L-HL]} \\
& & & \textbf{Default L (17)} &
\end{array}
$$

On the other hand, when the host is /HL/ (like the words in (39)), we have two inherent falling tones within the same prosodic word. In the tonal patterns of the cliticized forms, however, none of the Falling tones seems to have surfaced. My assumption is that only the /HL/ of the host (i.e., the first /HL/) survives in the cliticized form. In other words, Cogtse requires that each prosodic word only have one marked tone in the underlying representation. In order to achieve this special OCP effect,[15] it deletes the tone(s) after the first /HL/ within the same tonal domain, be it a prosodic word or a prosodic phrase.[16]

---

15 In autosegmental phonology (Clements & Keyser 1983; Goldsmith 1976; Hayes 1989; Hyman 1985; McCarthy 1979; 1981; Steriade 1982), the OCP is applied to restrict adjacent singly-linked melodies. The present study, however, applies the OCP rule particularly to adjacent Falling tones, which are doubly-linked melodies.

16 The definition of the prosodic phrase will be discussed in details in §0.

(42)**OCP Deletion:** Delete tone(s) after a /HL/ within the same tonal domain

Once a tone is associated to a syllable, it spreads rightward onto toneless syllables.

(43) **T-Spread:** A tone spreads rightward onto toneless syllables once it is associated to a syllable

As for why the first /HL/ does not surface as falling but as high level, related studies have shown that contour tones tend to be simplified in non-final position. Zhang (2002), in a survey of contour-tone distribution, figures that phrase-final syllables are preferred contour-bearers, and the pitch excursion of contour tones are greater on a final syllable than on the same syllable elsewhere. Based on this generalization, I assume that Cogtse does not allow non-final contours, so a potential non-final contour is avoided by deletion of the underlying L from /HL/. A contour-simplification rule is thus stated as in (44) for Cogtse:

(44) **Contour Simplification:** L is deleted from /HL/ if it is non-final

Consider the derivation in 58. OCP Deletion (42), T-spread (43) and Contour Simplification (44) are the first three rules to apply.

After they are all applied, every syllable is toned, thus no other tonal rule is applicable.

(45) 'musk deer (PL)': câ + =ɲê (Surface: [H-L]

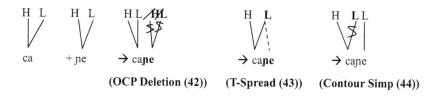

		ca	+ɲe	→ caɲe	→ caɲe	→ caɲe
				(OCP Deletion (42))	**(T-Spread (43))**	**(Contour Simp (44))**

In transcribing nominal plural and dual forms, I will represent the inherent tone values of both the host and the enclitic. For instance:

(46)

    a.   câ=ɲê (/HL/=/HL/)   'musk deer (PL)'
           musk.deer=PL

    b.   toru=ndʒês (/Ø/=/HL/   '(two) cats'
           cat=DU

The same tonal behavior induced by a non-final /HL/ is also seen in the third type of tonal interactions between words (§2.4.3).

2.3.3.1.3. Toneless Clitics

Toneless clitics include topicalizers =*tə*, =*mənaŋorə* and =*təmənaŋorə*, oblique topicalizer and subordinator =*ti*, as well as the ergative marker =*kə*. When these toneless enclitics are attached to the host, the last tone of the host spreads rightward onto the enclitics. Compare (47) and (48), which show how the topicalizer =*tə* receives different tonal values respectively from toneless and a falling-toned hosts. In (47), the postlexical tone pattern of *təpô* 'intestines' (/HL/) is [L-HL]. The encliticized noun phrase *təpô=tə* 'intestine=TOP' surfaces as [L-H-L] because the final tone of *təpô* (i.e., [L]) spreads onto the topicalizer, and non-final /HL/ is simplified.

(47) təpô + =tə 'intestine=TOP'   Surface: [L-H-L]

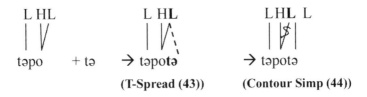

On the other hand, if the host is toneless and surfaces as [L-H] post-lexically, the enclitic =*tə* receives a H via the spread of the final tone of the host. For example:

(48) toru + =rə 'cat=TOP'　Surface: [L-H-H]

L H　　　　　　　L H　　　　N/A

toru　　+ tə　→ torutə

(T-Spread (43))　　**(Contour Simp (44))**

The tonal patterns observed on the topicalizer =tə are extendible to all the above-mentioned toneless enclitics.

2.3.3.2. Partial Tone Retention: Compounding

The only environment observed to involve partial retention of tone in this study is the formation of compounds. Irrespective of the tone of the other compound element, the compound normally surfaces with the tone of the second (i.e., rightmost) compound element.

(49)

  a.　/Ø/ + /Ø/ → /Ø/

    ta-me 'foot' + tə-mɲak[17] 'eye'

    → tamemɲak [L-H-H] 'ankle'

  b.　/Ø/ + /HL/ → /HL/

    tako 'head' + ɽɲê 'hair'

    → takoɽɲê [L-H-HL] 'hair'

---

[17] Prefixes tə- and ta- are nominal prefixes. They are removed if the noun stem they attach to is a non-initial element of a compound.

c. /HL/ + /Ø/ → /Ø/

smôn 'medicine' + ta-pat 'powder'

→ smonpat [L-H] 'powder medicine'

d. /HL/ + /HL/ → /HL/

təӡbâ 'face' + ʃɐɾɘ̂ 'bone'

→ təӡbaʃɐɾə [L-H-H-HL] 'cheek-bone'

2.3.3.3. Morphosyntactically-Assigned Tones

Three morphosyntactic environments have been observed to assign a specific tone irrespective of the inherent tone of the constituent morphemes. These morphosyntactic constituents are the Observational verb form (§2.3.3.3.1), the Indirect Evidential verb form (§2.3.3.3.2), and the Vocative case of nouns (§2.3.3.3.3).

2.3.3.3.1. Observational[18]

The Observational verb is formed with the observational prefix *na-(nɐ-)* and verb Stem1. In spite of the inherent tone of the verb, Observational verb forms are uniformly toneless. In other words, verbs that are inherently toneless remain toneless, while falling-toned verbs are deprived of their lexical tone and surface as toneless.

Note that the tonal rule is required by the grammatical

---

[18] The observational is an evidential category which indicates that an imperfective situation is witnessed at a certain point of its interval.

category to apply to the whole word. It is not the case that the observational prefix comes with a zero tone. Like the tonal assignment that occurs on the Indirect Evidential form, the grammar also assigns a tonal value to the whole Observational verb form, not just to the grammatical prefix in question.

In the following examples, the inherent tone of the verb is represented in its imperative form (thus on Surface-Melody 2). The Observational verb forms are also realized on Surface-Melody 2, but they are all toneless.

(50)

		Imperative		Observational	
a.	'stand'	to-rjap	(/Ø/)	na-rjap	/Ø/
		[H-L]		[H-L]	
b.	'release'	nɐ-lêt	(/HL/)	nɐ-lɐt	/Ø/
		[L-HL]		[H L]	
c.	'detour'	to-nə-pjol	(/Ø/)	na-nə-pjol	/Ø/
		[L-H-L]		[L-H-L]	
d.	'be sick'	to-nə-wô	(/HL/)	na-nə-wo	/Ø/
		[L-H-HL]		[L-H-L]	
e.	'put on top of another	to-sa-tak-tak	(/Ø/)	na-sa-tak-tak	/Ø/
		[L-H-H-L]		[L-H-H-L]	

	Imperative	Observational
f. 'read'	na-nə-mcɐ-rê (/HL/)	nɐ-nə-mcɐ-rɐw /Ø/
	[L-H-H-HL]	[L-H-H-L]

2.3.3.3.2. Indirect Evidential[19]

The segmental structuring and tone-placement rules involved in the Indirect Evidential verb vary for affirmative and negative meanings. The affirmative Indirect Evidential verb form, on the one hand, is composed of the indirect evidential past imperfective prefix *naa-* or one of the indirect evidential perfective prefixes[20] plus Stem1. Irrespective of the inherent tone of the verb, the affirmative Indirect Evidential form shows a uniform tone pattern in which the first two syllables are H, and the rest is L.[21]

---

[19] Indirect Evidential is a modal category which indicates that a situation, occurring before Speech Time, is not directly observed or perceived by the speaker (Cf. Y Lin 2000: §5.3).

[20] The indirect evidential perfective prefixes are formed by shifting the vowels of the seven orientationally specified perfective prefixes (*to-* 'upward', *na-* 'downward', *ko-* 'eastwards', *nə-* 'westwards', *ro-* 'upstream', *rə-* 'downstream', *jə-* (orientationally neutral)) to *aa-*.

[21] In X. Lin (1993), Hseih (1999), and Y. Lin (2000, 2003), the affirmative indirect evidential prefix is transcribed as monosyllabic instead of disyllabic (For example, the past imperfective indirect evidential prefix is *na-* instead of *naa-* in these previous studies). However, a further examination on this prefix in both elicited and spontaneous speech reveals that the indirect evidential prefix is disyllabic.

(51) Surface tonal patterns of Indirect Evidential forms

　　3 syllables　　　　　　　　4 or more syllables
　　H-H-L　　　　　　　　　**H-H-L-L...L**

The examples below show that both lexically toneless and falling-toned words surface uniformly with the affirmative Indirect Evidential tone pattern.

(52) 'to cry' /Ø/

　　a. Citation (with NOM *ka-*):　ka-ŋa-kru　**[L-H-H]**　　'to cry'
　　b. Indirect Evidential (PV):　ta-a-ŋa-kru　**[H-H-L-L]**　's/he cried'

(53) 'to be sick' /HL/

　　a. Citation (with NOM *ka-*):　ka-nəwo　　**[L-H-HL]**　'to be sick'
　　b. Indirect Evidential (PV):　ta-a-nə-wo　**[H-H-L-L]**　's/he got sick'

I assume that Affirmative Indirect Evidential assigns a Falling tone (/HL/) to the second syllable, irrespective of the underlying tonal value of the verb stem.

(54) **IE Tone Assignment (Affirmative):** The affirmative Indirect Evidential verb takes a /HL/ on the second syllable

After being associated to the second syllable, /HL/ breaks into a H-L sequence, and the tones spread respectively onto their neighboring toneless TBUs by T-Spread (43). And finally, the initial /HL/ undergoes Contour Simplification (44) (since it is situated at a non-final position), and the expected surface form is achieved. Take 's/he got sick (Indirect Evidential, Aff)' as an example:

(55) kə-nəwô 'to be sick'

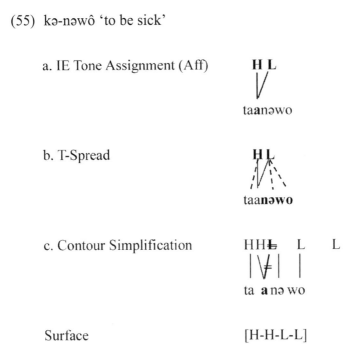

a. IE Tone Assignment (Aff)

b. T-Spread

c. Contour Simplification

Surface   [H-H-L-L]

The above processes give us the expected surface pattern: [H-H-L-L]. Affirmative Indirect Evidential verbs with toneless verb stems also undergo the same derivational process.

The negative Indirect Evidential verb, on the other hand, is composed of a negative prefix *mə-* followed by an indirect evidential prefix *ŋa-* plus verb stem (for both perfective and past imperfective situations):

(56) Negative Indirect Evidential (Perfective and Past Imperfective)

mə- + ŋa- + V
NEG- + EVI + VERB.STEM

Examples (57) and (58) compare affirmative and negative Indirect Evidentials. Note that the negative Indirect Evidentials are realized on distinct surface patterns from that of their affirmative counterparts.

(57) 'to cry' /Ø/

b. Indirect Evidential (PV):   ta-ŋakru   [**H-L-L**]   's/he cried'
c. Indirect Evidential (PV:NEG): mə-ta-ŋakru   [**H-L-L-L**]   's/he didn't cry'

(58) 'to be sick' /HL/

b. Indirect Evidential (PV):   ta-nəwo   [**H-L-L**]   's/he got sick'
c. Indirect Evidential (PV:NEG): mə-ta-nəwo   [**H-L-L-L**]   's/he didn't get sick'

These surface differences are assumed to have resulted from the fact that Zhuokeji morphology associates a /HL/ to the initial syllable of a negative Indirect Evidential verb:

(59) **IE Tone Assignment (Negative):** The affirmative
Indirect Evidential verb takes a /HL/ on the initial
syllable

After the application of this tone-assignment rule, rules of
T-spread (43) and Contour Simplification (44) are also needed
to derive the surface phonological representation. Take
mə̂ŋaŋakru 's/he didn't cry~s/he was not crying (Indirect
Evidential)' as an example:

(60) ka-ŋakru 'to cry'

a. IE Tone Assignment (Neg)

H L
/
məŋaŋakru

b. T-Spread

H L
/
məŋaŋakru

c. Contour Simplification

H L L L
/
mə ŋa ŋa kru

Surface

[H-L-L-L]

2.3.3.3.3. Vocative Case

As in Caodeng Rgyalrong (J. Sun 2007), most personal names in Cogtse are direct Tibetan loans. The following data show that the vocative forms of personal names can take either /Ø/ or /HL/, with the /HL/ assigned to the final syllable.

(61)

		Person Name		Vocative Form		
				/Ø/	~	/HL/
a.		kraʃes	/Ø/	kraʃes	~	kraʃês
		[L-H]		[H-L]	~	[L-HL]
b.		ptsɐsmôn	/HL/	ptsɐsmon	~	ptsɐsmôn
		[L-HL]		[H-L]	~	[L-HL]
c.		mtsʰomoscit	/Ø/	mtsʰomoscit	~	mtsʰomoscît
		[L-H-H]		[L-H-L]	~	[L-H-HL]
d.		kraʃismôn	/HL/	kraʃismon	~	kraʃismôn
		[L-H-HL]		[L-H-L]	~	[L-H-HL]
e.		kraʃiłamo	/Ø/	kraʃiłamo	~	kraʃiłamô
		[L-H-H-L]		[L-H-H-L]	~	[L-H-H-HL]

2.4. The Prosodic Phrase

The tone rules introduced in §2.3 are applied within, and therefore define the domain of the prosodic word. The domain of contrast between /HL/ and /Ø/ is not the syllable, but the whole word, and the tonal shape of a prosodic word can be derived by a set of tone rules. Beyond the domain of the word, on the other hand, tonal interactions are observed between prosodic words within a single prosodic phrase. In this study, a prosodic phrase is composed of one or more prosodic words. The prosodic phrase is defined by a set of tonal rules that has the prosodic phrase as its domain (§2.4.1-§2.4.3). It will be shown later in Chapter 3 that the intonation unit is composed of one or more prosodic phrases. Based on the Strict Layer Hypothesis (Nespor & Vogel 1986; Selkirk 1984), I am proposing the following prosodic hierarchy for Cogtse, in which an intonation unit is composed of one or more prosodic phrases (PP); each prosodic phrase must contain at least one prosodic word (PW), and each word must contain at least one foot. The foot is preferably binary.

(62) Cogtse Prosodic Hierarchy

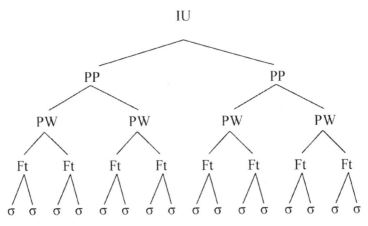

Specific tonal rules are applied within the domain of the prosodic phrase. A prosodic phrase can be composed of one or two words (in the absence of a prosodic accent). Based on the interactional behaviors between words, four types of tonal modifications are observed. Notably, each of the grammatical constructions examined below can only occur with one of the four interactional types. This suggests that tonal modifications on the phrasal level vary with the grammatical nature of the prosodic words within the prosodic phrase. Moreover, in these constructions, speakers can choose to pronounce the components as separate phrases or as a single phrase.

2.4.1. Phrasal Modifications: Type 1

The first type of phrasal modifications is observed in the Noun-Adjective phrase as exemplified in (63):

(63) Cogtse Noun-Adjective Phrases

a.	/Ø/ /Ø/	ʃkam kətsʰo	'fat muntjac'
b.	/Ø/ /HL/	ʃkam kəktê	'big muntjac'
c.	/HL/ /Ø/	kʰûŋ kətsʰo	'fat tiger'
d.	/HL/ /HL/	kʰûŋ kəktê	'big tiger'

In these constructions, the component can be pronounced in two ways. One is to treat the prosodic words as two distinct prosodic phrases, and so pronounce each of them with its own lexical melody (64a, 65a, 66a, 67a). In the other alternative realization, the first word maintains the lexical melody, while the second word switches to the phrase-final pattern (64b, 65b, 66b, 67b). If the first component is falling-toned, the non-final /HL/ is further simplified to /H/.

(64)

/Ø/ /Ø/		ʃkam kətsʰo	'fat muntjac'
⟶ a.	{H} {L-H}	
⟶ b.	{H H-L}	

(65)

/Ø/ /HL/		ʃkam kəktê	'big muntjac'
⟶ a.	{H} {L-HL}	
⟶ b.	{H H-HL}	

(66)

/HL/ /Ø/		kʰûŋ kətsʰo	'fat tiger'
⟶ a.	{HL} {L-H}	
⟶ b.	{H H-L}	

(67)

/HL/ /HL/		kʰûŋ kəktê	'big tiger'
⟶ a.	{HL} {L-HL}	
⟶ b.	{H H-HL}	

The data show that Cogtse seems to require a H-L sequence on a phrase-final element. That is, the penultimate syllable must be a H, and it should end with a L. Note that a word is phrase-final when it is preceded by one or more words within the same phrase and is followed by the phrasal boundary. When a word stands as a phrase by itself, although it is followed by the phrasal boundary, the rule of Phrase-Final H-L does not apply.

(68) **Phrase-Final H-L:** A phrase-final word should end with a H-L sequence if it is preceded by another word within the same phrase

The derivational process in (69) demonstrates how a phrase-final toneless word achieves its phrasal output.

(69)

toru kətsʰo 'fat cat' (/Ø/ /Ø/)

Lexical Output	L H L H
	toru kətsʰo

Phrase-Final H-L	L H **H** **L**
	toru **kətsʰo**
Output	[L-H H-L]

When the phrase-final word is falling-toned (/HL/), the rule of Phrase-Final H-L is applied, as well. However, as the falling-toned word (/HL/) already ends with a L, the requirement of H-L sequence is partially fulfilled by the final L. Therefore, the rule of Phrase-Final H-L only replaces the penultimate L with H, and the final /HL/ remains invariant. For example:

(70)

toru kəktê 'big cat' (/Ø/ /Ø/)

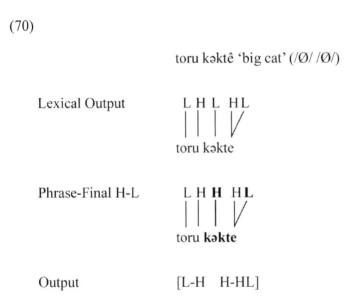

Lexical Output	L H L H L
	toru kəkte

Phrase-Final H-L	L H **H** H **L**
	toru **kəkte**

| Output | [L-H   H-HL] |

Even in situations in which the two components are falling-toned, no tone is deleted by OCP Deletion (42). The two words retain their own tonal value, with the second word switching to the phrase-final pattern, and the first HL simplified to [H].

(71)

/HL/ /HL/   rdəgə̂ kəktê   'big argali'
⟶   a.   {L-HL} {L-HL}
⟶   b.   {L-H   H-HL}

Consider the derivation in (72. No particular ordering is required with Contour Simplification (44) and Phrase-Final H-L (68).

(72)

rdəgə̂ kəktê 'big argali' (/HL/ /HL/)

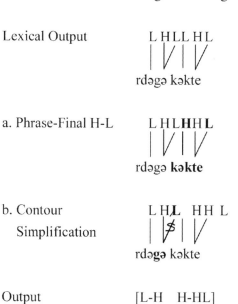

Lexical Output	L H LL H L
	rdəgə kəkte
a. Phrase-Final H-L	L H L H H L
	rdəgə **kəkte**
b. Contour Simplification	L H**L** H H L
	rdəgə kəkte
Output	[L-H H-HL]

However, there are cases for which there is no way to decide whether two words constitute a prosodic phrase. In these cases, the first word is toneless, and the second word is falling-toned and of three or more syllables. In such cases, even if the rule of Phrase-Final H-L (68) is applied, the falling-toned word surfaces with the same melody as its lexical output. Consider example (73):

(73)

tətʃi kəməʃtâk [water cold] 'cold water'(/HL/ /HL/)

Lexical Output	L H L H H L | | | | | ⁄ tətʃi kəməʃtak
Phrase-Final H-L	L H L **H** H **L** | | | | | ⁄ tətʃi kə**məʃtak**
Output	[L-H L-H-HL] (identical to the lexical output)

There is one more situation in which the first type of interactional modification does not occur. That is, when one of the words is of four or more syllables, there is no way for the two words to be produced as a single phrase. Consider example (74):

(74)

/Ø/ /Ø/   abururu kətsʰo   'fat snail'

⟶ a.   {L-H-H-L}

           {L-H}

⟶ b.   *{L-H-H-L

           H-L}

This seems to suggest that the head of a prosodic phrase should be no longer than three syllables. The longest phrase (or, rather, the longest combination that still shows phrasal modification) is composed of a trisyllabic head plus a trisyllabic final, as exemplified in (75) below:

(75)

/Ø/ /Ø/   tamdipu kəmago   [orphan stupid]

⟶ a.   {L-H-H   }   'stupid orphan

           {L-H-H}

⟶ b.   *{L-H-H

           L-H-L}

2.4.2. Phrasal Modifications: Type 2

The second type of interactional modification is observed in Noun-Numeral phrases, as shown below:

(76) Cogtse Noun-Numeral Phrases

a.	/∅/ /∅/	∫kam kə∫nəs	'seven muntjacs'
b.	/∅/ /HL/	∫kam kəmŋô	'five muntjacs'
c.	/HL/ /∅/	kʰûŋ kə∫nəs	'seven tigers'
d.	/HL/ /HL/	kʰûŋ kəmŋô	'five tigers'

In these constructions, the tonal value of the first element determines whether a binary prosodic phrase can be formed. If the first element is toneless, the construction can either be pronounced as one single prosodic phrase (77b, 78b), or as two distinct prosodic phrases (77a, 78a).

(77)

/∅/ /∅/   toru kə∫nəs   'seven cats'

         ⟶ a.   {L-H } {L-H }
         ⟶ b.   {L-H   H-L}

(78)

/∅/ /HL/   toru kəmŋô   'five cats'

         ⟶ a.   {L-H } {L-HL }
         ⟶ b.   {L-H   H-HL}

The examples above in (77b) and (78b) show that, when the first element is toneless, the phrase-final patterns are identical to the patterns that have been introduced for Phrasal-

Modification Type 1 (§2.4.1). In order to derive the correct output, the rule of Phrase-Final H-L (68) is applied. The derivations in (79)-(80) show respectively how a toneless (79) and a falling-toned word (80) obtain the observed phrase-final forms.

(79)

toru kəʃnəs 'seven cats' (/Ø/ /Ø/)

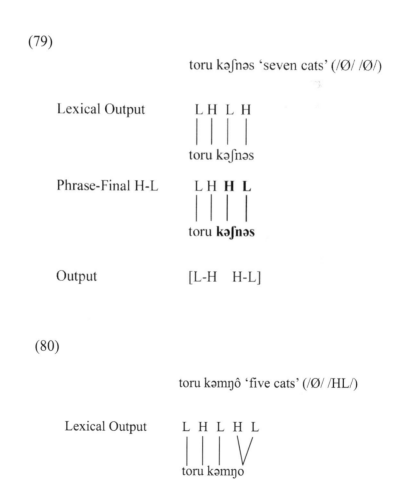

| Lexical Output | L H L H |
| | toru kəʃnəs |

| Phrase-Final H-L | L H **H L** |
| | toru **kəʃnəs** |

| Output | [L-H   H-L] |

(80)

toru kəmŋô 'five cats' (/Ø/ /HL/)

| Lexical Output | L H L H L |
| | toru kəmŋo |

Phrase-Final H-L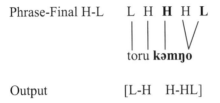

Output   [L-H   H-HL]

However, the present phrasal-modification type differs from Type 1 in one respect. That is, when the first element is /HL/, the two words must always reside in their own prosodic phrases:

(81) Noun-Numeral Phrases

/HL/ /Ø/		kʰûŋ kəʃnəs	'seven tigers'
	⟶	{HL } {L-H }	
		*{H H-L}	
/HL/ /HL/		kʰûŋ kəmŋô	'five tigers'
	⟶	{HL } {L-HL }	
		*{H H-HL}	

2.4.3. Phrasal Modifications: Type 3

The third type of interactional modification occurs in the possessive construction and the Noun-Verb phrase. The mechanism will first be introduced using examples of possessive constructions. Then, I will show that the same generalizations are applicable to the interactions observed in the Noun-Verb phrase.

The Cogtse possessive construction is represented by a prefix which indexes the possessor on the nominal roots, and the tonality of the whole construction is determined by the tonality of the root. For example:

(82) Basic possessive construction

	Noun			Possessive	
a.	ʃkam /Ø/	'muntjac'		ŋə-ʃkam	'my muntjac'
	[H]			[L-H]	
b.	toru /Ø/	'cat'		ŋə-toru	'my cat'
	[L-H]			[L-H-H]	
c.	kʰûŋ	'tiger'		wə-kʰûŋ	'his tiger'
	[HL]			[L-HL]	
d.	rdəgə̂	'argali'		wə-rdəgə̂	'his argali'
	[L-HL]			[L-H-HL]	

There exists an extended construction where the relevant possessor occurs in the form of a full noun or a pronoun (with full nouns mostly taking third person singular possessive prefix wə-). For example:

(83)

a. /Ø/ /Ø/ ʃkam wa-me 'muntjac's foot' [muntjac 3SG:POS-foot]

b. /Ø/ /HL/ ʃkam wə-rnâ 'muntjac's ear' [muntjac 3SG:POS-ear]

c. /HL/ /Ø/ kʰûŋ wa-me 'tiger's foot' [tiger 3SG:POS-foot]

d. /HL/ /HL/ kʰûŋ wa-rnâ 'tiger's ear' [tiger 3SG:POS-ear]

Speakers can treat the components of these phrases as two distinct prosodic phrases, and pronounce them with their lexical melody. See examples in (84):

(84) Possessive constructions (components in separate prosodic phrases)

a. /Ø/ /Ø/ ʃkam wa-me 'muntjac's foot' [muntjac 3SG:POS-foot]

⟶ {H} {L-H}

b. /Ø/ /HL/ ʃkam wə-rnâ 'muntjac's ear' [muntjac 3SG:POS-ear]

⟶ {H} {L-HL}

c. /HL/ /Ø/ kʰûŋ wa-me 'tiger's foot' [tiger 3SG:POS-foot]

⟶ {HL} {L-H}

d. /HL/ /HL/ kʰûŋ wa-rnâ 'tiger's ear' [tiger 3SG:POS-ear]

⟶ {HL} {L-H}

If the speaker is to treat the phrase as a single prosodic phrase, however, the tonal modifications involved are in principle determined by the tonal value of the first component of the phrase. To make it explicit, if the first word is toneless, then the inherent tone of the second component is retained, but surfaces with the phrase-final H-L. Compare the examples in (85) and (84a-b).

(85) Possessive constructions pronounced as one prosodic phrase

a. /Ø/ /Ø/ ʃkam wa-me 'muntjac's foot' [muntjac 3SG:POS-foot]

⟶ {H   H-L}

b. /Ø/ /HL/ ʃkam wə-rnâ 'muntjac's ear' [muntjac 3SG:POS-ear]

⟶ {H   H-HL}

On the other hand, if the first component has a lexically specified /HL/, then the first component surfaces with H, while every syllable following the /HL/ is uniformly realized as L. Compare (84c-d) with (86):

(86) Possessive constructions within one prosodic phrase (First component /HL/)

a. /HL/ /Ø/ kʰûŋ wa-me 'tiger's foot' [tiger 3SG:POS-foot]

⟶ {H   L-L}

b. /HL/ /HL/ kʰûŋ wa-rnâ 'tiger's ear' [tiger 3SG:POS-ear]

⟶ {H   L-L}

This is reminiscent of the tonal phenomena observed on Plural/Dual cliticization (§2.3.3.1.2). In fact, OCP Deletion (42), T-Spread (43), and Contour Simplification (44) do work here to derive the expected surface pattern for possessive constructions like those in (86). Note that lexically, only /HL/ is specified; but on the phrasal level, tonal rules are applied to the lexical output, in which /HL/, /L/, and /H/ are all specified. Tones after /HL/ are deleted even on the phrasal level, which suggests that /HL/ is still the most marked among the three tones. Taking 'elephant's ear' (87) as an example, OCP Deletion deletes all the tones after the first /HL/ (85a). Then, /HL/ spreads rightward onto toneless syllables resulting from OCP Deletion (87b). After non-final /HL/ is simplified to [H] (87c), the expected surface form is derived.

(87) laŋpotʃʰê 'elephant'   rnâ 'ear'

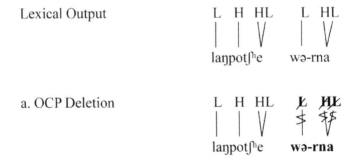

b. T-Spread

L H HL
| | /⌃⟍⟍⟍
laŋpotʃʰe **wə-rna**

c. Contour Simplification

L H H⌐L   L   L
| | \⌐ | |
laŋpotʃʰe   wə-rna

Surface

[L-H-H   L-L]

The same generalization is extendable to the Noun-Verb phrase, which is composed of a noun and a verb nominalized with *ka-*: [N   *ka-*V]

(88) Noun-Verb Phrases

a.	/Ø/ /Ø/	laɪga ka-pɑ	'to dance' ('dance' + 'to do')
b.	/Ø/ /HL/	ʃammdu kɐ-lêt	'to fire (a shot)' ('gun' + 'to release')
c.	/HL/ /Ø/	tsʰûŋ ka-pa	'to do business' ('business' + 'to do')
d.	/HL/ /HL/	soŋlâ kɐ-lêt	'to saw ('saw (n.)' + 'to release')

The tonal modifications are the same as those observed in the possessive constructions as shown above in (85) and (86). That is, if the first component is /Ø/, the second component retains its inherent tone; if the first component is /HL/, the second word only surfaces with L.

(89)

a.	/Ø/ /Ø/	targa ka-pa {L-H H-L}	'to dance' ('dance' + 'to do')
b.	/Ø/ /HL/	ʃammdu kɐ-lêt {L-H H-HL}	'to fire (a shot)' ('gun' + 'to release')
c.	/HL/ /Ø/	tsʰûŋ ka-pa {H L-L}	'to do business' ('business' + 'to do')
d.	/HL/ /HL/	soŋlâ kɐ-lêt {H L-L}	'to saw ('saw (n.)' + 'to release')

These data show that Cogtse Rgyalrong has nesting prosodic phrases. This particularly refers to the rules of T-Spread (43) and Initial Replacement, the latter of which will be discussed in §2.4.4. Consider the phrase *tsʰûŋ ka-pa=tə* [N+NMZL-V= TOPICALIZER]. The topicalizer here is an enclitic that gets its tone by a spreading of the final tone of the host. Instead of receiving a H via the spreading of the final tone of the nominalized verb *ka-pa* (i.e., [L-H]), the topicalizer receives a L. This is because the noun and the nominalized verb form a prosodic phrase in the first cycle, then the final tone of the

phrasal pattern [H-L-L] is spread onto the topicalizer in the
second cycle. See the demonstration of the process in (90):

(90) tsʰûŋ 'business' ka-pa 'to do

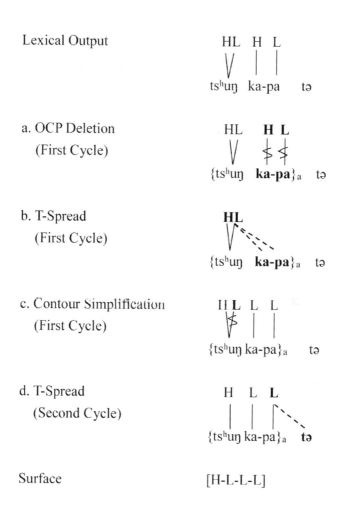

Lexical Output	HL H L
a. OCP Deletion (First Cycle)	HL **H L**
b. T-Spread (First Cycle)	**HL**
c. Contour Simplification (First Cycle)	H **L** L L
d. T-Spread (Second Cycle)	H L L
Surface	[H-L-L-L]

2 4 4. Phrasal Modifications: Type 4

The remaining type of phrasal modification can be observed on the finite verb and the word that immediately precedes it. When a finite verb forms a tonal phrase with the word that precedes it (usually a noun or an adverb), the initial tone of the finite verb is replaced by the final tone of the preceding word. Consider example (91):

(91)

kʰri	to-ntʃʰê-w		'S/he selected rice'
rice	PV-select-TR		
[H]	[L-HL]	→ {H	H-HL}

In this example, the noun *kʰri* 'rice' and the finite verb *tontʃʰêw* 'selected (PV)' are situated within one single phrase. The initial L tone of the finite verb is thus replaced with a H, which is spread from the final tone of the preceding noun *kʰri*, as illustrated below.

(92)

Lexical output

$$
\begin{array}{ccc}
\text{H} & \text{L} & \text{H L} \\
| & | & \vee \\
\end{array}
$$

kʰri tontʃʰew

Initial Replacement

H ↙ H L

k^hri **tontʃ^hew**

Surface [H   H-HL]

In example (93) *təjnô nɐstsuw* 'S/he selected vegetables', a toneless finite verb *nɐstsuw* 'select (PV)' forms a prosodic phrase with a falling-toned noun *təjnô* 'vegetables' that precedes it. In such cases, the final L tone of the noun/adverb first spreads rightward and replaces the initial tone of the verb (93a). Then, the non-final /HL/ is simplified to [H] (93b) to derive the surface form.

(93)

Lexical output

L H L H   L

təjnɔ nɐstsuw

a. Initial Replacement

L HL H   L

təjno **nɐstsuw**

b. Contour Simplification

L H LL   L

təjno nɐstsuw

Surface [L-H   L-L]

2.5. Summary and Discussion

I hope to have demonstrated that it is possible to characterize Cogtse word prosody in strictly tonal terms. The prosodic phenomena in Cogtse argue for a multi-layered model of prosodic structure that incorporates the syllable, word, foot, prosodic phrase. In the analysis, I propose that the Cogtse tone system exhibits a tonal contrast between /Ø/ and /HL/. Only /HL/ must be specified in the lexicon, then the surface melody of both falling-toned and toneless words can be derived by a number of tonal, especially foot-parsing and tone-assignment rules. The surface realization of /Ø/ is sensitive to distinct grammatical contexts where it is situated, and must be realized with either Surface-Melody 1 or Surface-Melody 2 depending on different contexts. A switch in the ordering of the foot-parsing rule can account for the two different surface melodies.

Related linguistic facts that justify the assumption of a privative tone system (/HL, Ø/) for Cogtse are shown throughout §2.3-2.4, codified here in (94).

(94)

    a   OCP Deletion deletes tones after a /HL/ in Cogtse, and not tones after a /Ø/.

        Examples:

  1. Plural/Dual Cliticization (§2.3.3.1.2)
  2. Prosodic-Phrase Modification Type 3 (§2.4.3)
 b   Morphological rules manipulate /HL/, and not /Ø/
     Example: Indirect Evidential (§2.3.3.3.2)
              vs. Stem1-Stem2 alternation (§2.3.3.1.1)
              (/HL/ can either occur word-initially or
     word-finally)
 c   When /Ø/ and /HL/ occur in the same word, the result is
     /HL/, not /Ø/.
     Example: Plural/Dual Cliticization (§2.3.3.1.2)

The Cogtse lexical tonal contrasts and grammatical tonal variations discussed in this tonal analysis are summarized in Table 2.2.

Lexicon:	/HL/ vs. /Ø/
Stem1-Stem2 Alternation:	Tonal polarity of /HL/ and /Ø/
Compounds (two-component):	Tonal value of the second component
Observational:	/Ø/
Indirect Evidential:	Initial /HL/
Vocative case (noun):	/Ø/ or /HL/

Table 2.2 Cogtse lexical tonal contrast and grammatical variations

In generative phonology, there has always been a research strategy by which underlying forms should be "minimally redundant" (Kiparsky 1982), and all predictable phonological behaviors should be accounted for by conventions, rules, or constraints. The present strictly tonal analysis of Cogtse word prosody follows this strategy by assuming a privative tonal system of /HL/ vs. /Ø/. It not only avoids analytical and typological problems that a tone and pitch-accent approach may raise, but also provides a simpler and more coherent tonal picture throughout lexicon and grammar. In particular, while a tone and pitch-accent approach must specify /H/, /HL/, /*/ on distinct locations for different grammatical constructions, the present account handles the same facts with a more restricted inventory of tonal entities /HL, Ø/. More importantly, now we can clearly see that the lexical contrast between /HL/ and /Ø/ is adhered to in the grammar (see Stem1-Stem2 alternation of verb, for instance). In a tone and pitch-accent analysis, the same contrast is represented with an underlying /HL/ versus a rather unmotivated penultimate /*/.

Up to this stage, and based on all the information we have obtained about Cogtse word prosody, it should be appropriate to identify Cogtse as a tone language that contrasts /HL/ and /Ø/ generally within the domain of the word. The tonal system, albeit restricted to some extent, is not only used to contrast lexical meanings, but also is exploited for morphosyntactic purposes.

Chapter 3
Intonation Units: Segmentation and Intonation

3.0. Introduction

The present study is based on the assumption that speech flow can be naturally segmented using prosodic features into intonation units. Chafe (1987) characterizes the IU as "a sequence of words combined under a single, coherent intonation contour", and hypothesizes that the IU represents a speaker's focus of consciousness, a minimal unit of thought organization. Park (2002), based on this hypothesis, discovers that the intonation unit is not only a unit of cognitive processing, but also a resource speakers can maneuver for achieving their interactional goals.

This chapter will start with the identification of IUs by means of six prosodic cues (coherent intonation, pause, reset, anacrusis, final lengthening, and creakiness) in §3.1, then move to the internal analysis of intonation contours within IUs thus identified in §3.2) It will be demonstrated that Cogtse intonation can be appropriately described using three prosodic parameters: phrasal rules, prosodic accents, and a final boundary tone H%. Section 3.3 summarizes the analyses proposed in this chapter and addresses the issue of transitional continuity as a direction for future research.

3.1. Labeling IU Boundaries

In this study, IUs are defined perceptually. In the following subsection (§3.1.1) I will introduce the auditory prosodic criteria for IU-boundary identification. Inter-rater reliability tests were carried out to secure the reliability of the segmentation of data in this study. Section 3.1.2 will give an account of the methodology and results of the tests.

3.1.1. Prosodic Criteria for IU-boundary Identification

Intonation is not the only prosodic cue one can rely on to identify IU boundaries. Cruttenden (Cruttenden 1997: 42) suggests that one or both of the following 'external' criteria should be used to identify unit boundaries: (i) change of pitch level or pitch direction of unaccented syllables; (ii) pause, and/or anacrusis, and/or final syllable lengthening, plus the presence of a prosodic accent in each part-utterance thus created. Du Bois et al. (1992; 1993), on the other hand, propose five prosodic cues for IU identification: coherent contour, pitch reset (beginning of the unit), pause (between units), anacrusis (beginning of the unit), and lengthening (end of the unit). These prosodic cues are mostly adopted from Cruttenden's (1997) set of criteria. A major difference is that Du Bois et al. take 'coherent contour' as one of the primary cues; while Cruttenden (1997: 36) thinks ideally one should use the other four cues to identify the boundary, and only use an "internal criterion" like coherent contour when none of the other "external criteria" is applicable.

The present study adopts most of the prosodic cues introduced in Du Bois et al. (1992; 1993) and Cruttenden (1997) (namely pause, coherent intonation, pitch reset, anacrusis, and final lengthening) to identify the boundaries between IUs in Cogtse. Meanwhile, creakiness was also observed to occur quite frequently at IU-final position, and therefore is included as an IU-boundary cue. Table 3.1 summarizes all the boundary cues, their prosodic characteristics, and in which part of the IU (i.e., beginning, end, or the whole IU) they tend to occur.

Prosodic Cues	Characteristics	Location (IU)	Notes
1. Coherent Intonation	Unified intonation contour, fluid transitions between highs and lows without interruption	Whole IU	
2. Pause	(Nearly) zero energy	Between IUs	A pause in fact occurs between two IUs. However in this study pauses are consistently marked at IU-initial positions.

Prosodic Cues	Characteristics	Location (IU)	Notes
3. Reset	A resetting of pitch to a higher level	Beginning	The beginning of an IU may get higher in pitch than the end of the previous IU.
4. Anacrusis	Accelerated speech rate	Beginning	
5. Final lengthening	Decelerated speech rate	End	Vowel lengthening is not phonemic in Cogtse.
6. Creakiness	Laryngealization of creaky voice	End	Sometimes in fast speech, creakiness can be carried through from the end of an IU to the beginning of following IU.

Table 3.1 Prosodic cues for IU-boundary identification in Cogtse

These criteria were employed to segment the narratives into IUs. As stated in §1.0, the present study is grounded in the assumption that prosody and grammar are two distinct levels of speech organization. Therefore, syntax is not considered in any case of IU identification, as suggested by Du Bois et al. (1992; 1993). Most of the time the segmentation is quite straightforward, yet there are still difficult cases that do not display very clear prosodic cues. I found it helpful to compare these cases with IU prototypes to make a proper judgment.

3.1.2. Inter-Rater Reliability Tests

A series of inter-rater reliability tests was undertaken for the prosodic segmentation. The purpose was to determine whether the methodology was appropriate and could be applied consistently by different raters. An additional transcriber was recruited to test the boundary cues. This other transcriber (henceforth SR) is a native speaker of Mandarin Chinese who does not know the Rgyalrong language, and had no prior training in speech science or prosodic labeling. The fact that the transcriber does not know the Rgyalrong language helps avoid syntactic and semantic bias in prosodic segmentation.

Approximately 10% of the data (twelve minutes in total) were drawn from the dataset for the inter-rater reliability test. Two minutes were taken from each of the six speakers' contributions.

The tests were conducted in two phases. The first phase includes all boundary cues but intonation contour. Between the two phases, the author examined all the narratives in the database, selecting all the IUs that do not rely on intonation as the sole boundary cue, then moved to the internal analysis of pitch patterns with IUs thus chosen. The second phase started after a comprehensive analysis of Cogtse intonation was obtained, and the prosodic cue of coherent intonation could be identified based on specific phonological features.

To start off, the rater was first provided with stretches of recorded speech segmented into intonation units, with the boundary cues evident for each IU noted. The materials were edited and displayed using sound and TextGrid in Praat, as illustrated in Figure 3.1 A sample of the training material for the inter-rater reliability test. At this stage, she was instructed on all boundary cues except intonation contour.

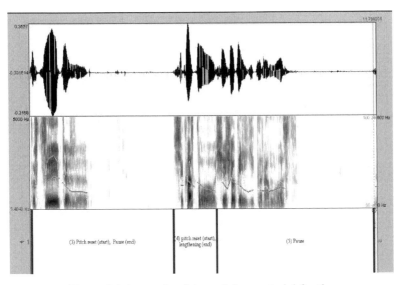

Figure 3.1 A sample of the training material for the
inter-rater reliability test

The rater was told to work through several examples of this type until she felt confident she understood the boundary cues and why the segmentation was made. She was then provided with unsegmented stretches similar to the examples she had just studied. She was asked to segment them and to note the boundary cues which formed the basis for the segmentation. Notice that although Praat provides visual-auditory cues, the rater was told to use only the auditory one. I also provided my own segmentation and notation cues for the same stretches of speech. We then compared the number of prosodic-unit boundaries marked respectively by the two transcribers. Both the location of the boundaries and the boundary cues were examined. The results of this phase of the study will be discussed below.

Before the second phase of the study, I conducted an analysis of the unit contour shapes. I then introduced SR to the notion of unit contour shape, presenting her with clear examples of rises and falls from outside the data set. Without having access to her decisions and notation from the first phase, SR was then asked to re-segment the same set of data, but this time including contour information as one of the boundary cues. The segmentations of the author and the rater were then compared again and analyzed.

In summary, the prosodic analysis procedure was broken down into five stages:

1) Boundary cues identified by the author (Segmentation Phase 1)

2) Inter-transcriber consistency (Segmentation Phase 1)
3) Intonational analysis by the author
4) Boundary cues identified by the author (Segmentation Phase 2)
5) Inter-transcriber consistency (Segmentation Phase 2)

In the first phase, both raters divided the excerpts into IUs based on all the prosodic cues except intonation contour, yielding the following agreement rate:

Number of IU boundaries marked by the author	404
Number of IU boundaries marked by SR	358
Number of identical IU boundaries marker by SR and the author	309
Agreement rate	309/404= 76%

Table 3.2 Agreement rate (Inter-rater reliability test, Phase 1)

Adding the intonational analysis as one of the boundary cues, the author and SR segmented the same dataset again. This time a high agreement rate was achieved.

Number of IU boundaries marked by the author	402
Number of IU boundaries marked by SR	387

Number of identical IU boundaries marker by SR and the author	356
Agreement rate	356/402= 89%

Table 3.3 Agreement rate (Inter-rater reliability test, Phase 2)

After the reliability of the prosodic cues was secured, the author went on to re-segment all the narratives into IUs. The twenty narratives were divided into 3,253 IUs. Among the prosodic cues, intonation contour is by far the most frequent (roughly 93%).[1] Pitch reset is also very common. Roughly 64% of the IUs start with pitch reset. More than half of the IUs (58%) have a pause at the beginning. Final lengthening occurs in 28% of the IUs. About 6% of the IUs display anacrusis. Finally, creakiness occurs in 3% of the IUs.

3.2. Intonational Analysis

We now turn to one of the primary goals of this study, an examination of the roles of tone and intonation in determining the overall contour shapes of IUs. In the present study, I use the term "intonation" to refer to phonological structures of phrase and utterance level which are represented by specific pitch patterns. Intonation in this sense is close in spirit to what Ladd defines as "the use of suprasegmental phonetic features to

---

1   Among the IUs segmented in the present study, about 7% are truncated, and therefore do not bear a coherent contour of their own.

convey 'postlexical' or sentence-level pragmatic meanings in a linguistically structured way" (1996: 6). While tone is a phonological feature of lexical items and is largely fixed and predictable, intonation varies with the discourse and pragmatic meanings denoted by the units to which tones are associated.

The primary data come from spontaneous narratives, supplemented by isolated examples recorded for various contexts (i.e., yes-no interrogatives, content interrogatives, declaratives, citations, utterance medial elements, and focused elements). The narratives were initially segmented into IUs. Intonation was analyzed using concepts and methods adopted from the autosegmental/metrical (AM) theory. The analysis started with a segmental transcription, including the marking of phrasal boundaries. The segmental analysis was then compared to pitch trace produced by Praat to determine whether the variation in F0 can be appropriately characterized by the transcription.

The results strongly suggest that three parameters are sufficient to account for Cogtse intonation: phrasal rules (§3.2.1), prosodic accent (§3.2.2), and the boundary tone H% (§3.2.3). The assignment of the boundary tone and the specification of phrasal boundaries and prosodic accents are not specified in the lexicon and can barely be predicted by phonological rules.[2] Rather, the operation and placement of these phonological tones are determined by postlexical and discourse-level meanings intended by the speaker, which goes in line with the definition of "intonation" proposed by Ladd (1996: 6). The following subsections will demonstrate how the three parameters operate and interact to achieve the surface intonational contours observed.

3.2.1. Phrasal Rules

The contour shape of an IU is not a combined sequence of all the word tones within. However, in many cases, it seems adequate to say that in Cogtse, the contour shape of an IU reflects the combined sequence of all the tones within it (lexical tones, modified by phrasal rules).

The Cogtse prosodic phrase can be composed of one or more words, and is defined by a set of tonal rules that specify the head and phrase-final melodies. Table 3.4 summarizes four types of modifications observed in six primary phrasal constructions in the language (for more details see §2.4).

---

2 Some patterns in Type 2 phrasal modifications are exceptions. In Type 2, when the first element is falling toned, the word never forms a phrase with the word that follows. It is therefore possible to predict phrase parsing for Type 2 by the tonal value of the first element, without considering the contextual discourse meanings.

TYPE 1: NOUN + MODIFIER

Tonal Components	Phrasal Rules	Sample Patterns (disyllabic)	Sample Patterns (triyllabic)
/∅/ /∅/	Phrase-final H-L	/L-H/ + /L-H/ → [{L-H **H-L**}]	/L-H-H/ + /L-H-H/ → [{L-H-H**L-H-L**}]
/∅/ /**HL**/	Phrase-final H-L	/L-H/ + /L-HL/ → [{L-H **H-HL**}]	/L-H-H/ + /L-H-HL/ → [{L-H-H L-H-HL}] (same as lexical output)
/**HL**/ /∅/	Phrase-final H-L	/L-HL/ + /L-H/ → [{L-H **H-L**}]	/L-H-HL/ + /L-H-H/ → [{L-H-H **L-H-L**}]
/**HL**/ /**HL**/	Phrase-final H-L	/L-HL/ + /L-HL/ → [{L-H **H-HL**}]	/L-H-HL/ + /L-H-HL/ → [{L-H-HL-H-HL}] (same as lexical output)

TYPE 2: NOUN + NUMERAL

Tonal Components	Phrasal Rules	Sample Patterns (disyllabic)	Sample Patterns (triyllabic)
/∅/ /∅/	Phrase-final H-L	/L-H/ + /L-H/ → [{L-H **H-L**}]	/L-H-H/ + /L-H-H/ → [{L-H-H**L-H-L**}]
/∅/ /**HL**/	Phrase-final H-L	/L-H/ + /L-HL/ → [{L-H **H-HL**}]	/L-H-H/ + /L-H-HL/ → [{L-H-H L-H-HL}] (same as lexical output)
/**HL**/ /∅/	N/A (never a phrase)	/L-HL/ + /L-H/ → [{L-H} {L-H}]	/L-H-HL/ + /L-H-H/ → [{L-H-H} {L-H-H}] (same as lexical output)
/**HL**/ /**HL**/	N/A (never a phrase)	/L-HL/ + /L-HL/ → [{L-H} {L-HL}]	/L-H-HL/ + /L-H-HL/ → [{L-H-H} {L-H-HL}]

TYPE 3: POSSESSIVE AND [NOUN +NMZL-VERB] PHRASES

Tonal Components	Phrasal Rules	Sample Patterns (disyllabic)	Sample Patterns (triyllabic)
/∅/ /∅/	Phrase-final H-L	/L-H/ + /L-H/ → [{L-H **H-L**}]	/L-H-H/ + /L-H-H/ → [{L-H-H**L-H-L**}]
/∅/ /HL/	Phrase-final H-L	/L-H/ + /L-HL/ → [{L-H **H-HL**}]	/L-H-H/ + /L-H-HL/ → [{L-H-H L-H-HL}] (same as lexical output)
/HL/ /∅/	OCP Deletion	/L-HL/ + /L-H/ → [{L-H L-L}]	/L-H-HL/ + /L-H-H/ → [{L-H-H **L-L-L**}]
/HL/ /HL/	OCP Deletion	/L-HL/ + /L-HL/ → [{L-H L-L}]	/L-H-HL/ + /L-H-HL/ → [{L-H-H**L-L-L**}]

TYPE 4: [NOUN/ADVERB FINITE VERB]

Tonal Components	Phrasal Rules	Sample Patterns (disyllabic)	Sample Patterns (triyllabic)
/∅/ /∅/	Initial Replacement	/L-H/ + /H-L/ → [{L-H H-L}] (same as lexical output)	/L-H-H/ + /L-H-L/ → [{L-H-H**H-H-L**}]
/∅/ /HL/	Initial Replacement	/L-H/ + /L-HL/ → [{L-H **H-HL**}]	/L-H-H/ + /L-H-HL/ → [{L-H-H **H-H-HL**}]
/HL/ /∅/	Initial Replacement	/L-HL/ + /H-L/ → [{L-H **L-L**}]	/L-H-HL/ + /L-H-L/ → [{L-H-H L-H-L}] (same as lexical output)
/HL/ /HL/	Initial Replacement	/L-HL/ + /L-HL/ → [{L-H L-HL}] (same as lexical output)	/L-H-HL/ + /L-H-HL/ → [{L-H-HL-H-HL}] (same as lexical output)

Table 3.4 Types of phrasal modifications observed in six
major phrasal constructions

Table 3.4 shows that in Types 1, 2, and 3, the phrase-final word must have a H-L sequence at the end if it is preceded by a toneless (/∅/) word. On the other hand, when the first word is falling-toned, Types 1 and 3 respectively resort to Phrase-Final H-L and OCP Deletion to mark the domain of the phrase; while in Type 2, the falling-toned initial word never forms a phrase with any word that comes after it. In Type 4, despite the tone value of the words, the post-lexical output of the first word always spreads its final tone rightward, and replaces the initial tone of the following word if both words are situated in the same phrasal domain.

By demonstrating phrase parsing and its related phrasal-tone rules in (95), I show that the pitch contour of the IU below is directly derived from the tones of all the prosodic phrases that make up the IU.

(96) Narrative07 IU_49

{tɐntsət tə}ₐ {ŋa}ᵦ {ɹɐspɐ nawaroŋ ptʂe}꜀ {wuɲe todz̩əŋ}d

tɐntsət=tə	ŋa	ɹɐspɐ	na-warô-ŋ		ptʂe	wəɲê	to-dz̩ə̂t-ŋ
bullet=TOP	1SG	more	IMPFV:PST-have₂-1SG		then	those	PV-carry₂-1SG

'I had more bullets, so I carried them with me'

The IU in (96) is parsed into four prosodic phrases (a, b, c, and d) based on the tonal behaviors observed. The phrasal-rule modifications are briefly illustrated below.

(97) Phrasal Modifications in Example (96)

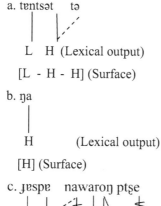

a. tɐntsət   tə   Toneless enclitic =tə receives a H

   L   H (Lexical output)   from the spreading of the final

   [L - H - H] (Surface)   tone of the host tɐntsət [L-H]

b. ŋa   N/A

   H   (Lexical output)

   [H] (Surface)

c. ɟɐspɐ   nawaroŋ ptşe   Phrasal rule Type 4: The initial L

   L H   L H HL   H   tone of the finite verb nawaroŋ is

   (Lexical Output)   replaced with a H, spread from
                             the final tone of the preceding
                             adverb ɟɐspɐ. The H of the
   [L.-H   H- H-H   L]   adverb ptse is deleted because its
   (Surface)   preceding word has a marked
                             tone /HL/. The adverb is then
                             produced with a default L.

d. wuɲe   todʐəŋ   Phrasal rule Type 4: The initial

   L HL L   HL   tone of the finite verb todʐəŋ is

   (Lexical Output)   replaced with a L, spread from
                             the final tone of the preceding
                             noun wuɲe. Because the initial
   [L-H   L- HL]   tone of todʐəŋ is also L, the
   (Surface)   surface melody of this word
                             remains invariant.

Compare the surface melody of the phrases with the pitch track of the IU in Figure 3.2 F0 track of Example (96). The combined phrasal output correctly characterizes the pitch movement of the IU.

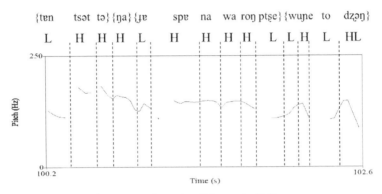

Figure 3.2 F0 track of Example (96)

Examples (98) and (99) contrast two situations of toneless words at the IU-final position. In (98) the ton ɛss nominalized verb (*ka-sə-ntap*) forms a prosodic phrase by itself, and thus remains on Melody 1 ([L-H-H]).

(98) Narrative02

54. ptşe³ {təmɲa təmənao} **{kasəntap}**

---

3   The adverb *ptşe* in this example is an unparsed word. A number of IUs start with a monotonous sequence of low tones as does this example. Such words or sequences seem to have been deprived of their lexical tones, and show no pitch movement for the examination of phrasal rules; they are therefore left unparsed in the intonational analysis. In other words, in the prosodic transcription, all unparsed words are on low tone.

ptşê	tə-mɲa=təmənaŋorə	ka-sə-ntap
then	N-field=TOP	NMZL:GP-CAUS-be.flat₁

'then (we) flatten the field'

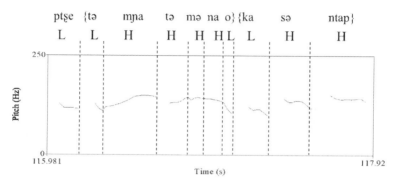

Example (99), on the other hand, demonstrates a typical [Noun NMZL-Verb] phrase in which both words are toneless (Type 3).

Example (99), on the other hand, demonstrates a typical [Noun NMZL-Verb] phrase in which both words are toneless (Type 3)..

(99) Narrative02

83. {takpa kapa}

ta-kpa	ka-pa
N-sheaf	NMZL:PL-do₁

'(men) sheaf (the grain)

The second word (*ka-pa*) forms a phrase with the noun that

precedes it, and thus ends with Phrase-Final H-L.

(100) Phrasal modification in example (101)

ta-kpa   ka-pa

[L-H]   +   [L-H]   →   [L-H **H-L**]

Consider the pitch track of this IU:

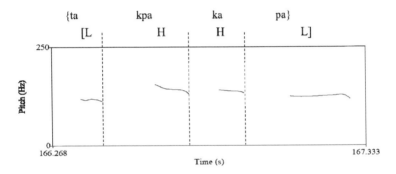

Figure 3.4 F0 track of Example (99)

One should not expect the [Noun NMZL-Verb] construction to always be produced as one unified phrase in prosodic terms. In fact, all the phrasal rules summarized above in Table 3.1 are only applicable when speakers choose to produce two words as though in one prosodic phrase. Otherwise, the words can also be treated as residing in separate phrases. The alternation appears to be largely context-dependent. Example (101) shows a case in which a falling-toned nominalized verb (*ka-rə-rô*) forms a prosodic phrase by itself. If the noun *nəɲɑ̂ɲê* 'milk cows' and the nominalized verb formed a prosodic phrase, by phrasal modification Type 3 the nominalized verb should be deprived of its falling tone by OCP Deletion and surface with default Ls. However, the situation observed is that *ka-rə-rô* ([L-H-HL]) retains all of its post-lexical tones, which means the verb forms a prosodic phrase by itself.

(101)   Narrative04

     23. {nəŋaɲe} {karəro}
           nəŋâ=ɲê   ka-rərô
           milk.cow=PL   NMZL:GP-look.after₁

     '(we) look after milk cows'

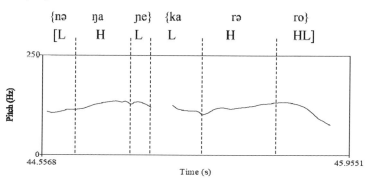

Figure 3.5 F0 track of Example (101)

Example (102) illustrates a case of phrase-nesting in Cogtse. The IU has two prosodic phrases, with one phrase nested within the other.

(102) Narrative04

26. {{wupsokɲe kapa}ₐ naŋos}ᵦ
wəpsôk=ɲê   ka-pa l   na-ŋôs
that.way=PL NMZL:GP-do₁IMPFV:PST-COP₂

'(we) did things like that'

The IU is parsed from left to right, and *wupsôkɲê* and *kapa* form a phrase before the resulting phrase builds up a phrase with *naŋôs*. In other words, the parsing comes in two cycles. In the first cycle, the post-lexical tones of *kapa* [L-H] are deleted by OCP Deletion since they are preceded by a falling tone in the same prosodic phrase (Modification Type 3).

(103) First Parsing Cycle of the IU in (104) [4]

{wupsôkɲê²⁶   kapa}
  | | | ‡ ‡
  L H L   L H

The phrase {*wupsokɲe kapa*} surfaces as [L-H-L L-L] after the first cycle, with *kapa* being realized with default Ls. Then, {*wupsokɲe kapa*} forms a phrase with *naŋôs*, and the final tone of *kapa* (i.e., output of the first cycle, now L instead of H)

---

4 The falling tone on *psok* is realized as H since it occurs non-finally.

spreads rightward and replaces the initial tone of *naŋos*.

(104) Second Parsing Cycle of the IU in (104)

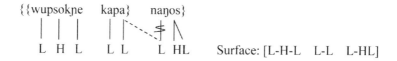

Surface: [L-H-L   L-L   L-HL]

Compare the phrasal melody with the F0 tracking of the IU in Figure 3.6. The phrasal output again correctly characterizes the pitch movement of the IU.

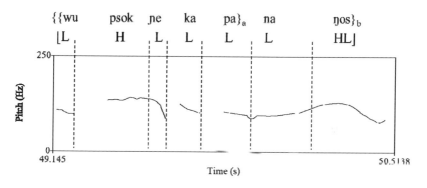

Figure 3.6 F0 track of Example (102)

3.2.2. Prosodic Accent

Cogtse has prosodic accent, which is defined by its phonological behavior rather than any phonetic features that are commonly used to define prominence. The prominence of Cogtse prosodic accent is determined by the fact that every syllable after it must surface as low. Therefore, if the prosodic accent is IU-medial, one would see a gradual fall after the prosodic accent. Consider Example (105), in which the prosodic accent falls on the second syllable of the verb *roˆtʰɐj* (the accent is marked with a "ˆ" at the beginning of the accented syllable). The following subordinator/oblique topicalizer =*ti*, topicalizer =*mənaŋorə* and the adverbial *atô* 'upstream' all surface with default Ls. The pitch track of the IU shows a gradual fall from the accented syllable till the end.

(105) Narrative07

66. {**roˆtʰɐ=j** ti mənaŋorə ato}
     ro-tʰɐl-j=ti=mənaŋorə   atô
     PV:upstream-go₂-1PL=SUB=TOP upstream

'When we went upstream'

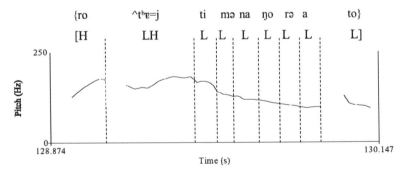

Figure 3.7 F0 track of Example (105)

The surface realizations of the prosodic accent vary with the length of the accented syllable. That is to say, if the accented syllable is short, the prosodic accent surfaces as high level. In the example below, a prosodic pitch-accent falls on the second syllable of *tǝjnô* 'dish (food)', putting every syllable after it on L. In this case the accented syllable is short, and the accent is realized as high level.

(106)   Narrative04

23. {tǝ^jno kapa kǝkʰut ɲeɲe tǝ}

tǝ-jnô   ka-pa   kǝ-kʰut=ɲeɲê=tǝ
N-dish(food)   NMZL-make   NMZL-be.allowed₁=PL=TOP

'those (mushrooms) that can be served at table'

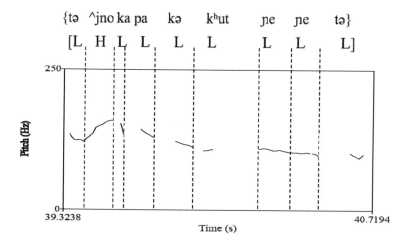

Figure 3.8 F0 track of Example (106)

On the other hand, the prosodic accent is usually realized as rising if the accented syllable is elongated. For example, the IU in (107) has a prosodic pitch-accent on the last syllable of *tʂəlapʰak-j* 'half way-LOC'. The accented syllable is elongated, and is realized as rising.

(107) Narrative05

68. {**tʂəla^pʰa=j** tosamdu ti mənaŋorə}

     tʂəlapʰak=j   to-sa-mdu=ti=mənaŋorə

     half.way=LOC   PV-PL-arrive₂=SUB=TOP

'when (we) get to the halfway point'

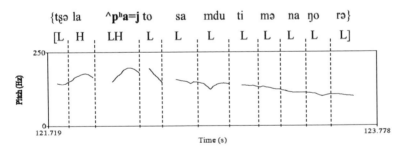

Figure 3.9 F0 track of Example

If the prosodic accent were not there, the final tone of tʂəlapʰak-j [L-H-H] could spread rightward and replace the initial tone of the finite verb (Modification Type 4). The surface melody of the phrase {tʂəlapʰaj tosamdu} would be [L-H-H H-H-L]. Nonetheless, since the IU has the prosodic accent on *pʰaj*, the finite verb is deprived of all the tonal values and surfaces with default Ls.

As also shown above in (107) and (108), words that come after the prosodic accent are analyzed as being located in the same prosodic phrase with the accented word. While in most cases an IU can have only one prosodic pitch-accent, it is possible for an IU to have two, as the example below illustrates.

(109) Narrative07

37. {nɐkə^ŋkʰɐ=n nɐk^tsə=s nɐtsə}
     nɐ-kə-ŋkʰɐn   nɐ-kə-tsəs   nɐ-tsəs
     OBV-NMZ-be.many[1]   OBV-PL-say[1]   OBV-say[1]

'"They said there are many (deer)" he said'

The pitch track in Figure 3.10 shows that both accents are realized as rising, with the latter rising more steeply (and being longer) than the former one.

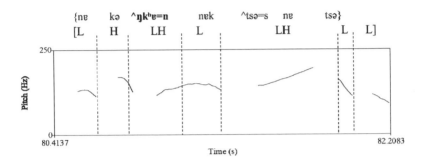

Figure 3.10 F0 track of Example (109)

3.2.3. Boundary Tone

Cog... has only one boundary tone: H%. It is something speaker can choose to use, but it is also phonologically constrained. That is, the boundary tone can only be realized on final low tones that result from prosodic-phrase modifications and/or the placement of prosodic accent. H% is realized as rising irrespective of the length of the IU-final syllable. Contrast the following examples for the absence (111) and presence (110) of H%. In (111), all the syllables in the topicalizer =təmənaɲorə receive a low tone via the spreading of the final tone of kʰaʃʰâ 'deer' [L-HL].[5] The pitch of the IU therefore drops from the beginning of the topicalizer through the end:

5　For the analysis of toneless clitics, cf. §0.

(111)   Narrative07

117.   {kʰaʃa təmənaŋorə}
kʰaʃâ=təmənaŋorə
deer=TOP

'(as for) deer'

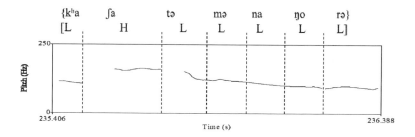

Figure 3.11 F0 track of Example (111)

Note again that the terminal direction in (111) is not due to the higher level intonational structure, but just results from the application of phrasal rules. Example (111) demonstrates an example without H%, (112) illustrates the presence of the boundary tone. Example (112) is again composed of a falling-toned noun (*tanâp* 'morning') followed by the toneless enclitic topicalizer *=təmənaŋorə*. The pitch drops from the first syllable of *=təmənaŋorə* until before the last syllable, which rises because of the presence of the boundary tone, H%.

(112) Narrative06

9. {tanap təmənaŋorə=} H%
ta-nâp=təmənaŋorə
N-morning=TOP

'(as for) the morning'

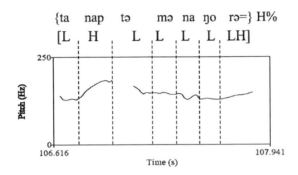

Figure 3.12 F0 track of Example (112)

As mentioned at the beginning of this subsection, the boundary tone is realized as rising on both short and long syllables. In other words, the rising contour of H% is not a concomitant prosodic feature of final prolongation.

The function of the boundary tone is yet to be fully determined. However, the contexts where H% is used suggest that the boundary tone is not regularly associated with any particular grammatical construction. Indeed, the elicited data collected for this study show that, if ending with a toneless syllable, questions tend to end with low tone (113), and declaratives tend to have a rising terminal contour (114):[6]

(113) Elicitation_YDF--- Question

{wəjo}{ kʰri stsû-w mə}

wəjo   kʰri   stsû-w   mə

3SG   rice   pound₁:NPST-TR   Q

'Will he pound rice?'

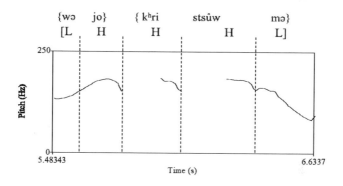

Figure 3.13 F0 track of Example (113)

(114) Elicitation_YDF--- Declarative

{wujo} {təjnô nɐ-stsu-w}H%

wəjo   təjnô   nɐ-stsu-w

3SG   vegetables   OBV-pound₁-TR

---

6 A similar prosody-grammar correlation is also observed in Chickasaw by Gordon (2005). Chickasaw speakers often end statements with a final rise, and questions (both yes-no and wh-) with a low tone.

'He has pounded vegetables'

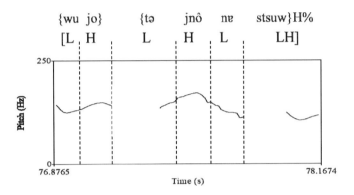

Figure 3.14 F0 track of Example (114)

Nonetheless, in spontaneous speech, the opposite co-occurrences are heard frequently as well. That is, questions can end with a rising contour (115), and declaratives can have a terminal low (116).

(117) Narrative16

83. {kondon mə} H%
ko-tə-ndô-n   mə
IMPFV:self.person-2-there.be₂-2SG   Q
'Are you (still) there?'

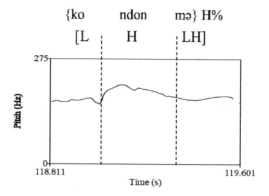

Figure 3.15 F0 track of Example (117)

(118) Narrative16

20. {kənəzjɐk totsos}

kənəzjɐ̂k   to-tso-s

the.second.night   PV-elapse₂-s

'The second night passed'

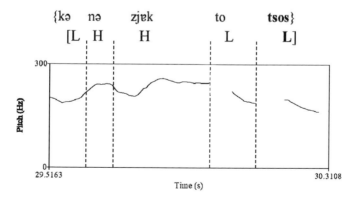

Figure 3.16 F0 track of Example (118)

The distribution of the boundary tone seems to suggest that H% denotes some discourse-functional meaning. Below are the distributional features of the boundary tone in all the narratives examined.

Distributional Feature 1: Frequent occurrence with vocative nouns. The vocative case can switch every noun (toneless or falling-toned) to toneless Melody 2, so that every vocative noun ends with a low tone (cf. §2.3.3.3 for detail), and, therefore, susceptible of the realization of H%. Consider example (119) and its pitch track. The utterance is produced by a beggar who was calling one of the daughters of a farm owner.

(119) Narrative13

    77. {ŋɐʃimi} {ŋɐʃimi} H%
        ŋɐ-ʃimi   ŋɐ-ʃimi
        1SG:POS—Miss:VOC 1SG:POS-Miss:VOC
    'Miss, Miss'

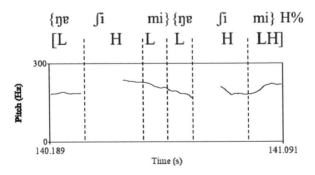

Figure 3.17 F0 track of Example (119)

It should be kept in mind, however, that the occurrence of this boundary tone is optional for contexts like this. There are also vocative nouns that are not realized with H%. The IU in (120) has exactly the same vocative nouns as (121), but it ends with a low tone instead of H%.

(122) Narrative13

269. {ŋɐʃimi} {ŋɐʃimi}
      ŋɐ-ʃimi   ŋɐ-ʃimi
      1SG:POS- Miss:VOC   1SG:POS- Miss:VOC

'Miss, Miss'

{ŋɐ ʃi mi} {ŋɐʃi mi}
[L   H, L, L, H , L]

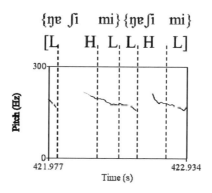

Figure 3.18 F0 track of Example (122)

Distributional Feature 2: Hesitation, stage holding. Hesitation markers like *mm* or *e* are toneless in Cogtse. They frequently occur with a rising contour, which I assume is due to the occurrence of the boundary tone H%.

Distributional Feature 3: Prayer opening. In summoning a deity, speakers would say *mtʃʰomtʃʰomtʃʰot* to start their prayers. This prayer opening almost always has a rising terminal contour, as demonstrated in example (123):

(123) Narrative13

71. {^mtʃʰomtʃʰomtʃʰo=t}H%
mtʃʰomtʃʰomtʃʰot
(prayer.opening)

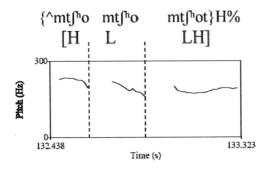

Figure 3.19 F0 track of Example (123)

Distributional Feature 4: Toneless imperatives. Toneless imperatives surface on Melody 2 (cf. §2.3.2 and §2.3.3.1.1 for detail), and the terminal contour can be either rising or low. The IU in (124) ends with a toneless imperative with H%.

(124) Narrative19

47. a {ɲo tə} {adi koŋapkin}H%

a	ɲo=tə	adî	**ko-ŋapki-ɲ**
PART	2SG=TOP	west	**IMP-hide₂(v.i.)-2PL**

'You (pl.) hide in the west'

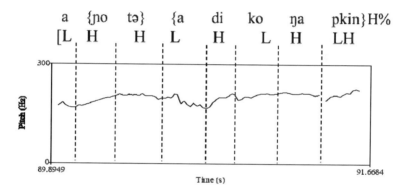

Figure 3.20 F0 track of Example (124)

Contrast the example above with (127), the latter of which has an imperative ending in a low tone.

(125) Narrative10

63. {wutə nasjok}

wətə	**na-sjok**
that	**IMP-finish₁**

'Finish reading that'

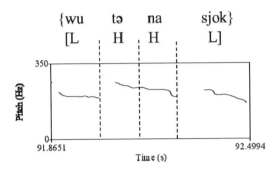

Figure 3.21 F0 track of Example (125)

The presence of H% at the end of imperatives seems to show politeness, as if to attenuate the directive quality of the command to more of a suggestion or advice. The imperative with H% in (124), for example, was uttered by a man to his colleagues. Example (125), ending with a low tone, was said by a monk to his apprentice. Nonetheless, there seems to be no way to discern such a distinction on falling-toned imperatives, which stays invariantly falling-toned in all contexts.

Distributional Feature 5: Attention appealing. The boundary tone also seems to be employed when the speaker is saying something that could be surprising or of interest to the listener. For example, before starting a story, a speaker told my main consultant that she was not sure whether she could contribute a good story, as she has forgotten many good ones, and the statement ends with a rising contour.

(126) Narrative12

26. {kəsɐjməs ŋkʰɐn} %H
    kə-sɐ-jmə̂s   ŋkʰɛ̂n
    NMZL-1-forget₁   be.many₁:NPST

'I forgot many (stories) (lit. (stories) that I forget are many'

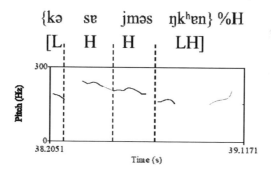

Figure 3.22 F0 track of Example (126)

<u>Distributional Feature 6</u>: The end of a narrative. If a narrative is about the speaker's own past experience, it usually ends with a specific expression: *wəpsôkɲê napsôt* 'It was like that'. This narrative-closing expression can have a prosodic pitch-accent on the second syllable of *wəpsôkɲê* , causing the pitch after the accent to drop gradually through the rest of the IU. In the narratives collected for this study, however, this pitch-accented expression always ends with a rising contour, as illustrated in (127).

(127) Narrative04

204. {wu^psokɲe napso=t} %H
    wəpsôk=ɲê   na-psôt
    that.way=PL   IMPFV:PST-be.like₂

'It was like that'

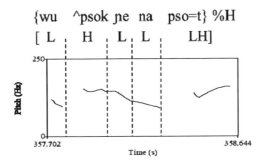

Figure 3.23 F0 track of Example (127)

As mentioned at the beginning of this subsection, H% is only realized on IUs ending with L. IUs ending with post-phrasal H or HL are pronounced as is. Example (128) demonstrates an IU that ends with a post-phrasal HL (Modification Type 4):

(129) Narrative07

61. tʂe {wuɲe todzɨj}
    ptʂê   wəɲê   **to-dzə̂t-j**
    then   those   **PV-take₂-1PL**

'then (we) took those (horses with saddles)

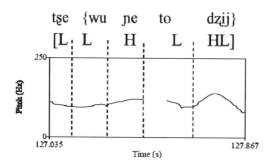

Figure 3.24 F0 track of Example (129)

If the pitch range gets low and the final syllable is lengthened, an IU-final post-phrasal HL is usually pronounced with a Rise-Fall pattern. Consider example (130) and its F0 track. The second syllable of *naŋôs* is elongated, and its post-phrasal falling tone surfaces as Rise-Fall.

(130) Narrative07

54. {{^tʂoɲʃotʂʰaŋ kɐtsəs} tə} {{wujo wuwɐj} nɐkərme} naŋo=s}
    tʂoɲʃotʂʰâŋ   kɐ-tsɔ̂s=tə
    breeding.stock.center   NMZL:GP-say1=TOP
    wəjo   wə-wɐ=j   nɐ-kə-rmê-j   **na-ŋôs**
    3SG   3SG:POS-PLACE=LOC   PV-NMZL-sleep₂-1PL **IMPFV:PST-COP₂**

'(a place) called Breeding Stock Center, there at his place we slept'

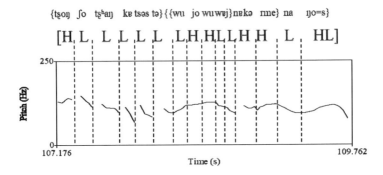

Figure 3.25 F0 track of Example (130)

In example (131), the toneless instrumental enclitic =kə receives a H tone from the spreading of the final tone of the adverb *tsotsos* [L-H]. The prosodic phrase that constitutes the IU ends with a post-phrasal H, and the IU therefore ends with a high level tone, as demonstrated below in Figure 3.26.

(131) Narrative07

25. e {tsotsos kə}

e   tsotsos=kə

PART often=INST

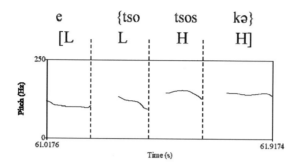

Figure 3.26 F0 track of Example (131)

To summarize, in Cogtse four surface terminal tones (high level, falling, low level, and rising) are observed at the end of the IU, but there is only one boundary tone (H%). The boundary tone surfaces as rising on IUs ending with a post-phrasal low tone. All the other surface terminal tones are post-phrasal tones of the IU-final word:

Post-Phrasal Tone	Boundary Tone	Surface Terminal
H	Ø	H
HL	Ø	HL
L	Ø	L
L	H%	LH

Table 3.5 Cogtse surface terminal directions and the interactions between the boundary tone H% and the three post-phrasal tones

3.3. Summary and Discussion

This chapter has presented the segmentation of speech flow into IUs, and has proposed a phonological analysis of pitch contours within the IUs. The present analysis claims that Cogtse intonation is not "overlaid" upon an IU for discourse-functional reasons. Based on an autosegmental/metrical (AM) approach, it has been revealed that the final pitch shape of an IU results from the interaction between the lexical tones, phrasal rules, prosodic accent, and the boundary tone H%. The proposed phonological model allows us to expect that the pitch shape of an IU is predictable if one knows the parsing of prosodic phrases, and the placement of prosodic pitch-accent(s) and the boundary tone; and that expectation is born out in all the examples adduced in §3.2. The analysis does not always apply transparently, and there are a number of difficult cases, especially when the pitch range of the intonation is reduced, and some pitch movements in an IU are not easy to discern. Nonetheless, the present approach should be an appropriate framework to account for the variations of IU contour shapes in Cogtse.

One of the central issues addressed in the prosodic studies by Chafe (1987; 1993) and Du Bois et al. (1992; 1993) concerns the transitional continuity categories. Chafe and Du Bois et al. observe that at the end of an IU, the speaker usually uses contour shapes to indicate whether his/her speech will continue or has finished. They suggest that probably all languages make intonational distinctions between the following transitional continuity classes: final (when the speech has finished), continuing (when the speech will continue), and appeal (when a speaker seeks a validating response from a listener). In other words, every language uses prosodic cues to signal speakers' intention for further speech.

At this stage, the configuration of Cogtse IU contours has been figured out, and it has been demonstrated with ample evidence that the surface IU contours are the result of the operation and placement of three phonological features. In other words, the intonational variations, especially the different terminal pitch directions observed in Cogtse, are not associated to the above-mentioned transitional-continuity classes.

In fact, Du Bois et al. (1993) are aware that the marking of finality can be language-specific and does not have to be restricted to terminal pitch directions. However, for the present study, the problem still remains as to how to identify "speaker's intention for further speech". It could be possible for people involved in conversation analysis to use potential turn transition relevance places as implications for discourse completeness (Ford & Thompson 1996). Nonetheless, the present study is based on monologic narratives, and very little interactional information can be obtained.[7] Owing to the limitation of the data, the issue of transitional continuity will have to await further research as more interactional information becomes available.

---

[7] Personal communication with Carol Genetti.

Chapter 4
Intonation Units: Grammatical Structure

4.0. Introduction

This chapter presents a grammatical profile of Cogtse based on IUs in natural speech. It examines the grammatical taxonomy of each IU segmented using the prosodic methodology introduced in Chapter 3. The distribution of the structural categories identified will be discussed against the context of related theoretical assumptions and generalizations proposed in previous related literature.

One of the most frequently addressed issues in studies of prosody-grammar alignment is that of the preferred syntactic structure of IUs. Based on spontaneous discourse data, Chafe (1987; 1994) discovers that the most recurrent IU type in American English is the clause. The proportion of clausal IUs is observed to be consistently higher than that of non-clausal IUs. In Mandarin Chinese, on the other hand, the clausal IUs do not form a predominant type. In his study of IUs in spontaneous conversations in Mandarin Chinese, Tao (1996) shows that the average proportion of clausal intonation units is just 47.9% in his database.

The differences in the proportion and predominance of the clause over the IU can be attributed to typological distinctions in grammar, as in the above-mentioned studies of English and Mandarin Chinese. Meanwhile, it can also be the result of different methodological criteria applied to define "clause" in studies of the same language. Japanese, for example, appears to fall between the clause-predominant and the non-clause-predominant extremes that are respectively represented by English and Mandarin Chinese. Iwasaki and Tao (1993), on the one hand, reported that the proportion of clausal IUs out of the 756 IUs examined is 45%. Matsumoto (2003), on the other hand, finds a much higher proportion (68%) out of the 1,600 IUs in her database. Matsumoto (2003) then compared these two studies on Japanese, and determined that the disparity between the results of the two studies stems from a major difference in research methods. That is, in Iwasaki and Tao (1993), only IUs with verbal predicate(s) are coded as clausal; while in Matsumoto (2003) clausal IUs can have both verbal and non-verbal predicate(s). In the present study, clausehood of Cogtse IUs are coded based on whether the IU has a verbal predicate or not (except for the two occurrences of verb-less clauses). Using a coding method similar to that applied by Tao (1996) and Iwasaki and Tao (1993), this study will determine the preferred syntactic structure of IUs in natural speech in Cogtse, a language that is typologically distinct from English, Mandarin Chinese, and Japanese.

Another major issue that will be addressed in the present

study is the tendency for each IU to contain no more than one clause. This tendency is noted by Chafe (1980) in Pear-Story narratives. It is assumed that each IU corresponds to one momentary focus of consciousness (Chafe 1994; 1996; 1998), which is roughly comparable to what Halliday refers to as "information unit" (Halliday 1985: 274). When the focus of consciousness involves an event or a state, it is usually represented in the form of a syntactic clause (Chafe 1997). Based on the assumption that speakers are able to verbalize no more than one new idea at a time (Chafe 1994; Halliday 1967; 1985), each clausal IU should ideally consist of no more than one clause (Chafe 1980; Halliday 1967).

The present study, however, will show that in Cogtse, the proportion of multi-clausal IUs is as high as 31%. This is much higher than the proportion of multi-clausal IUs coded by Croft (1995) for English, even after he restricts his clause types to finite main clauses.[1] Section 4.5.2 will discuss some possible reasons why these complex IUs may go against the "one clause one IU" tendency.

Some important and interesting research issues are related but will not be explored within the scope of the present study. One such issue concerns the distinction between full and

---

1 Croft (1995) in the same study further restricts the clause type to finite main clauses (That is, IUs with one finite main clause are mono-clausal, while IUs with two or more finite main clauses are multi-clausal).

elliptical clauses, i.e., whether the clausal arguments are overtly specified or elliptic. This topic is usually addressed as related to the "One Lexical Argument Constraint" as proposed by Du Bois (1987). Linguists examine which argument among A, S, and O would be elliptic under the constraint of "one new idea at a time" as suggested by Chafe (1987; 1994). The other issue concerns attachable and detached NPs. These are independent nominal IUs that are either integratable to a clausal structure (attachable NPs) or bear no structural relationship to any predicate in the adjacent IUs (detached NPs). These two issues are elaborated in IU studies by Tao (1996: , for Mandarin Chinese), and Matsumoto (2003: , for Japanese).

The main body of the chapter will start with evaluating some major discourse transcription systems before presenting the transcription conventions applied in this study on Cogtse (§4.1). Section 4.2 provides an account of the grammatical coding system, discussing how IUs are coded for grammatical types. The results of the grammatical study are provided in §4.3-§4.4. Section 4.3 describes all the structural types observed on the IUs. In particular, the cross-IU functional interpretations of the nominalized finite clause is examined and discussed in §4.3.2.1.2. Section 4.4, on the other hand, presents the distribution of these types. Section 4.5 provides a discussion of the results, focusing on the issue of the preferred syntactic structure and the nature and compositionality of multi-clausal

IUs. Section 4.6 describes two prosodic correlations to discourse and grammar respectively in extrapropositional expressions and the quotative construction. The findings presented in this chapter are summarized in §4.7.

4.1 Transcription System

4.1.1 Review of Some Major Transcription Systems

To transcribe Rgyalrong natural discourse and find an apt model to transcribe it is one of the major goals this study aims to achieve. It considers not only the design of a system to transcribe discourse data, but also what prosodic features to represent, and whether the system is typographically convenient.

Several systems designed to represent prosody in previous related studies have been considered. These systems include the intonational transcription system used in Bolinger (1989), INTSINT (Hirst & Di Cristo 1998), ToBI (Beckman & Ayers 1994; Beckman et al. 2005), the discourse transcription system used in Wennerstrom (2001), the discourse transcription system summarized in Du Bois et al. (1992; 1993), and a mixed system used by Genetti and Slater (2004) and Genetti (2007a; 2007b), which encompasses notations for both prosody and syntax.

The system used in Bolinger (1989) represents the pitch contour of a whole utterance. In the (English) transcription, letters are arranged like notes on a musical score. For example:

(132) (Bolinger 1989: 3)

```
               hó              pós           Just i
I want to go                It's im            má
                m                    sible.            sine!
                 e.
```

Such a representation is also reminiscent of the F0-tracing representations in speech-analysis programs, and it captures almost every pitch movement. It should be noted, however, that this system only represents two prosodic features, i.e., intonation and accent. Another limitation is that it is typographically inconvenient. To my knowledge, the musical-note-like arrangement of letters can hardly be done without having recourse to graphic programs.

The INTSINT (an International Transcription System for INTonation) was developed by Hirst and Di Cristo with the goal of accommodating all the possible variations of prosodic features across languages. It is like a narrow phonetic transcription of intonation, and thus can be applied in gathering data of intonational systems that are previously undescribed. In this model, intonational movements are represented using an array of pitch symbols on a separate line below each stretch of speech. For example:

(133)   (Hirst & Di Cristo 1998: 18, example (10))

I've	lost	more	patients	that	way!
[	→	⇑	>	⇓	↑]

This system is appropriate for those who are starting to collect intonational data in a new language. However, as Hirst and Di Cristo admit, INTSINT can only be used to transcribe pitch. The symbols applied to represent pitch movement are mostly special fonts, so the system is not typographically convenient. So far, people have only used it to represent utterances in isolation.

ToBI (Beckman & Ayers 1994; Beckman et al. 2005) is probably one of the most widely applied models for transcribing prosody. Recently there has been much interest in adapting this system to the transcription of languages other than American English (see all the studies in Jun (2005b)). A full ToBI transcription of an utterance contains at least six parts, each on a different layer: audio (waveform), F0 (pitch tracking), tones, words, break-indices, and miscellaneous. It is a very thorough system that represents many prosodic traits, and it works best for linguists involved in prosodic phonology, who wish to represent in the transcription the intonational configurations they have figured out, plus all the phonetic details they observe or use for analysis.

The model used in Wennerstrom (2001) was developed for

studying 'intonational meaning' in discourse. The system includes four main categories: pitch accents, pitch boundaries, key, and paratones. The space arrangement is nice for representing connected speech. In terms of typography, it is more convenient than the above-mentioned systems, although it also uses special arrows to mark pitch movement. This is a model that represents both prosody and discourse meaning. In example (134) below, an acute accent represents primary stress; the underlined capital letters indicate information contrasting with a prior idea or item in the discourse; subscripted capital letters indicate that the information is not new, and capital letters indicate that information being added to the discourse is new.

(134) (Wennerstrom 2001: 23)

um, the PRÍMARY ꜰᴜɴᴄᴛɪᴏɴ for the BÍCYCLE↘ in- (.) in the U.S.↗versus the ʙɪ́ᴄʏᴄʟᴇ in CHÍNA↓

The main reason why this model is not an apt choice for our purposes is that the goal of the present study is not to represent discourse meaning in the data. Even if discourse meaning is marked with notation in future studies, the system with capital and subscripted capital letters will not work for a language transcribed using IPA, where a roman letter and its capital counterpart (if available) represent distinct sounds.

The transcription framework summarized in Du Bois et al. (1992; 1993) is also one established for discourse transcription. The primary notations used in this system include those for unit boundary, speaker (for conversations), terminal pitch direction, transitional continuity (i.e., marking the speaker's intention to continue or finish his/her speech at the end of the IU, cf. §3.4 for more discussion), accent and lengthening, tone, pause, vocal noises, and voice quality. It is much more encompassing than the other systems mentioned above, except for the tracing of pitch movement. While INTSINT, for example, represents pitch movement of the whole utterance, the model of Du Bois et al only marks it at two locations in the IU-- the end of the unit, and the final primary accent. By using this model, one cannot transcribe transitional continuity before figuring out the functions of different contour types. However, this is overall a very useful system for discourse transcription. It is typographically convenient, as it avoids obscure fonts, and it can represent many prosodic features that are relevant to discourse analysis.

The model used in Genetti and Slater (2004), as well as Genetti (2007a; 2007b), is a variant of that is summarized in Du Bois et al. (1992; 1993), the difference being that Genetti and Slater use some different symbols for prosodic transcription, so that traditional morphological markings can be accommodated. For example, they use a colon (:) instead of the equal sign (=)

for lengthening, and save the equal sign for marking clitic boundaries. In their system, affix boundaries and word-final truncation are indicated by the same symbol-- a single dash (-). This, however, is not confusing since morpheme boundary only occurs in word-medial position, while the truncated word symbol only occurs word-finally. It is a compact system that represents both prosodic and morphological structures in one single transcription channel.

4.1.2. The Transcription System for Rgyalrong

In the present study, I use a system that transcribes prosody and morphology on separate levels. On the layer for prosodic and phonemic representation, the prosodic transcription basically follows the general approach of Du Bois et al (1992; 1993), with an additional marking of phrase boundaries. The morphological structure of the IU, on the other hand, is presented on a different line. Clarity is the major reason why this multi-layered system is adopted. Such a transcription system helps researchers tolook for prosodic and grammatical patterns to read the data more easily. The present study does not include the parameter of voice quality, vocal noise, and speaker overlap, so notations for these features are not included in the transcription system. However, since further discourse studies are being planned after the present project is completed, the model established at this stage should have the potential to include more prosodic and discourse-related notations in a convenient fashion. Such a multi-layered model is not very economical, but it can represent many real-time speech prosodic features as well as morphological information in a rather straightforward way. Table 4.1 summarizes this three-layered system:

Layer 1 Prosodic and phonemic representation
Layer 2 Morphological/phonological representation
Layer 3 Glossing

Table 4.1 The three-layered transcription system for Cogtse Rgyalrong

Layer 1 is the prosodic and phonemic representation. It transcribes what one hears in the recording, not only as "spurts of vocalization", but also all the related prosodic features, including pause, length, prosodic accent, and truncation that are observed within one "spurt". Also marked on this layer are phrase boundaries and pitch accent. Since most terminal directions can be predicted by phrasal parsing and prosodic accent placement, only the unpredictable boundary tone H% is marked on this layer. The markers of transitional continuity are not applied in the transcription, and the reasons are discussed in §3.4. The words are transcribed phonemically on this layer, and reduced forms are transcribed as produced. For example, if the word *na-kə-tsʰo* is reduced to *na-k-tsʰo* in natural speech, the word will be transcribed as [naktsʰo] on this level, leaving the morphological representation of the word (including tone) for Layer 2, the layer for the morphological and phonological representation. Following are the notations that will be used in the transcription.

1) Lengthened syllable or segment = equal sign
2) Accent (prosodic pitch-accent) ^ caret before accented syllable
3) Pause **(sec)** time in parentheses
4) Truncated word - dash at word-final
5) IU boundary carriage return
6) Phrase boundary { } phrase in curvy brackets
7) Word boundary space
8) Boundary tone H% / slash

Table 4.2 Notations for prosodic and phonemic transcription of Rgyalrong (Layer 1)

Layer 2 is the morphological/phonological transcription. The words are morphologically parsed and represented, with the lexical tone (/HL/) marked on the falling-toned vowel. Truncated words are not transcribed on this layer. The notations applied on the level are:

1) Morpheme boundary - dash between bound morphemes
2) Word boundary space
3) Clitic boundary = between the clitic and its host
4) Falling tone ^ circumflex on the falling-toned vowel

Table 4.3 Notations for morphological/phonological transcription (Layer 2)

Layer 3 is glossing. Glosses are left-aligned vertically with Layer 2, word by word. Segmentable morphemes are separated by hyphens, both in Layers 2 and 3. Finally, a free translation is provided when the meaning conveyed by a sequence of IUs can be translated into an English sentence.

Following is a transcription sample, which demonstrates how the data in this study are transcribed.

(135)   Transcription sample: an excerpt from Narrative05

1. {ŋəɲe} {ʃti=}
   ŋəɲê   ʃti
   1PL   here

2. (.8) {roŋmbɐsɐtʃʰej mənaorə=}
   roŋmbɐsɐtʃʰê̂=j=mənaŋorə
   Rgyalrong.area=LOC=TOP

3. (1.0) {kə^rtsu=j ptʂerə}
   kərtsû=j   ptʂêrə
   winter-LOC   then

4. (.5){ ʃi^kʰa sto=}
   ʃikʰâ   stô
   woods   upwards

5. (.6) {ʃe ^ʃo kɐjʒgi kəra ŋos}/
   ʃe=ʃô   kɐ-j-ʒgˁ   kə-râ   ŋôs
   firewood=usuallyNMZL-go.and-collect₁NMZL-be.necessary₁COP₁:NPST

IUs 1-5: 'Here in the Rgyalrong area, during the winter, it is necessary to go up to the woods to collect firewood'

4.2. Methodology: Coding Grammatical Types of the IU

The approach of grammatical coding applied in this study is close in spirit to Tao's (1996) in that it is "minimalistic". Instead of including larger prosodic- grammatical units like "extended clauses" (Chafe 1980; 1987) or "prosodic sentences" (Genetti 2007a; Genetti & Slater 2004), the present study investigates the grammatical exponent of each single IU independently.

Below are the six coding criteria:

Criterion ①: The domain for coding is restricted to single IUs. Even if an IU may form a larger grammatical unit with adjacent IUs, it is coded based on its own grammatical exponent, irrespective of its relation with the adjacent IUs. Consider example (136):

(136) Narrative03

23. (1.1) ptʂe {minpi=n}
     ptʂê   minpîn
     then   militia

24. (1.0) {nɐkʃin wuŋkʰuj} {jinəjaz wuŋˆkʰuj= mənaŋorə}
    nɐ-kʃin=wəŋkʰuj   jə-nəjâ-s=wəŋkʰuj=mənaŋorə
    PV-complete=after   PV-come/go.home₂-PST=after=TOP

IUs 23-24: 'After he was done with militia service, after he
came home'

The noun *minpin* 'militia' in IU23 forms a clause with the first
verb of IU24 (*nɐ-kʃin* 'PV-complete'). However, since they
appear in separate IUs, IU23 is coded as a nominal IU, while
IU24 is an IU of multiple adverbial clauses.

**Criterion ②: If the grammatical type of the current IU
could be altered when the following IU is considered, the
decision is still made based on the grammatical taxonomy of
the current IU.** In other words, the grammatical content of the
next IU is not considered at all. This criterion is particularly set
for parts of a direct quotes that are separated into various IUs,
as well as nominalized finite clauses. The present study first
codes these grammatical structure grounded on Criterion ②.
Then, while describing the structural types, the various cross-IU
interpretations of the nominalized finite clause are examined.
Examples (137) and (138) show that nominalized finite clauses
could be interpreted as serving grammatically distinct functions
if the following IU were considered. IU6 in example (137) and
IU152 in example (138) are both composed of a nominalized
verb attached by an oblique topicalizer =*ti*. If IU7 of example

(137) were considered for the coding of IU6, then IU6 would be interpreted as a headless relative clause.

(137) Narrative08

→   6. (0.5) {didi kə} {kəjam=ti}
didî=kə   kə-jâm=ti
gradually=INST   NMZL-be.wide₁=TOP:OBL

'(The place where the road) is wider and wider'

7. (0.5) {<x> sə^stoŋ ti nəkəkʃut nəŋo}
sʋstôŋ=ti   nə-kə-kʃût   nə-ŋos
wasteland=TOP:OBL   PV-NMZL-come.out₂   OBV-COP₁

'(He) came out to a wasteland'

By the same token, if IU153 of example (138) were taken into account, IU152 would be identified as a temporal adverbial clause:

(138) Narrative18

→ 152. (0.5) {kəjam kəstsə^stsə= ti ptʂe}
kəjam   kə-stsəstsə̂=ti   ptʂe
sun   NMZL-be.hot₁:REDU=TOP:OBL   then

153. {təmu ^rəwɹir napu ptṣe}

tə-mû	râw-ɟir	nâ-pɐ-w	ptṣê
N-weather	as.soon.as/right.away-change	PV:EVI-do₁-TR	then

IUs 152-153: 'While it was sunny and hot, the weather suddenly changed'

Nonetheless, in the first stage of grammatical coding, the adjacent IUs would not be considered. Consequently, IU6 of example (137) and IU152 of example (138) are both coded as nominalized finite clauses based on their common morphosyntactic structuring.

In example (139) below, we see an IU constituting a nominalized finite clause ending with a topicalizer =tə (IU6). If the following IUs (IU7 and IU8) were taken into account, IU6 would be recognized as a complement clause, with its CTP (*pʃetpê kɐ-lêt* 'to talk about') located one IU away in IU8:

(139) Narrative07

    5. {tɐrwɐk} nɐ=kə-
       tɐ-rwɐk
       N-hunting

→   6. {nɐkəpɐŋ tə=}
       nɐ-kə-pê-ŋ=tə
       IMPFV:PST-NMZL-do-1SG=TOP

7. {wutə tə=}
   wətə=tə
   that=TOP

8. {pʃet^pɐ te kɐlɐt} {ŋo=s}
   pʃetpễ   te   kɐ-lêt   ŋô̂s
   chat,talk   one   NMZL:PL-put   COP

IUs 5-8: 'That I did hunting (at Long'erjia), I will talk about that'

However, instead of doing so, IU6 is again coded as a nominalized finite clause, for the topicalizer =tə is not exclusively a complementizer in Cogtse. Consider example (140) for another use of the nominalized finite clause plus topicalizer =tə.

(140) Narrative11

→   65. {ndʒo} {^ste kətʃatʃ tə}/
       ndʒo   stê   kə-tʃâ-tʃ=tə
       1DU   so.very   NMZL-be.destitute₁-1DU=TOP

66.   {məˆɲe ste kəmaʃeɲ tə} {ndʒo dʒeʃij x}
      {kənəgaɲe makˆpo= toktsis nəŋo}

məɲê	stê	kə-maʃê-ɲ=tə		ndʒo	ndʒɐ-ʃî=j
3PL	so.very	NMZL-be.rich₁-2/3PL=TOP1DU		1DU	1DU:POS-place=LOC
kə-nəgal=ɲe		ma-kə-po		to-kə-tsis	nə-ŋos
NMZL-be.guest.to.a		NEG-PL-come₁		PV-NMZ-say₂	OBV-COP₁
feast₁=PL					

IUs 65-66: 'Since we are so very destitute, and they are so
very rich, they won't come and be our guests'

In IU65, the topicalizer =tə does not make the clause a
complement to any verbs in IU66. In fact, if IU66 were
considered for the coding of IU65, one would probably
interpret IU65 as an adverbial clause.

The examples presented so far show that the Cogtse
nominalized finite clause can be open to relative-clause, comple-
mentclause, as well as adverbial-clause interpretations,
depending on the context. At this stage, IUs constituted of the
nominalized finite clause are first coded based on its formal
structuring. Then, all the syntactic relationships that the
nominalized finite clause has to their surrounding contexts are
discussed in §4.3.2.1.2.

   **Criterion ③: If an IU consists of two or more elements
of the same non-clausal grammatical type, the IU will be
coded based on the structural type of these elements.** The

number of tokens of the coded type will not be considered. For instance:

(141) Narrative08

→ 133. (0.5) {tʂəlazdi} {wumbro}
    tʂəla=zdi   wə-mbro
    road=westsards   3SG:POS-horse

134. {kə^wdi nakətʃʰɐt nəŋo}
    kəwdî   nâ-kə-tʃʰɐt   nə-ŋos
    four   PV:EVI-PL-be.exhausted₂   OBV-COP₁

'On the road towards the west, his four horses got exhausted'

There are two nouns in IU133, and neither is a nominal predicate. The IU is therefore coded as a nominal IU, irrespective of the number of nominals in it.

Criterion ④ : Clausal IUs are coded based on morphosyntactic parameters including finiteness, nominalization, and complexity. All clausal types identified in the database will be described in §4.3.2.

Criterion ⑤: When an IU consists of two or more heterogeneous constituents that do not make up a larger

constituent, it is coded as a "disjoint" IU.[2] Consider example
(142):

(142) Narrative11

42. {kə^tʃɐntʃə= wutʃʰis kə}
    kə-tʃâ-ntʃ   wə-tʃʰîs=kə
    NMZL-be.destitute₁-2/3DU   3SG:POS-reason=INST

    'because they are destitute'

→ 43. ptʂerə raŋpas ptʂerə
     ptʂêrə   raŋpas   ptʂêrə
     then   especially   then

     'especially (destitute) then'

IU43 in the example consists of two connectives *ptʂêrə* 'then'
and an adverbial *raŋpas* 'especially', which du not bear any
direct syntactic relationship to each other. The unit is therefore
coded as disjoint.

As is also observed by Croft (1995: 859-860) in the
disjoint IUs in English, disjoint IUs in Cogtse can consist of
two elements that do not constitute a constituent themselves but
make up a clause with a preceding or following IU. Example
(143) demonstrates an IU like this.

---

2 The term and notion of "disjoint IU" are adopted from Croft (1995).

(143) Narrative03

18. {jo} {kəruʒimkʰam mənaŋorə} {pʰanlwan}
jo   kəru-ʒimkʰâm=mənaŋorə   pʰánlwan
1PL   Tibetan-Area=TOP   revolt(Chinese.loan)

→ 19. (1.1) kərwɐs tə ptʂerə wətətɲeɲe tə
 kə-rwês=tə   ptʂêrə   wəti=ɲeɲê=tə
NMZL-rise₁=TOP   then   there=PL= TOP

20. (0.6) e=
e
FIL

21. (0.2) {ˆtʃʰe kəra} {naŋos} ptʂerə
tʃʰê   kə-râ   na-ŋôs   ptʂêrə
go₁   NMZL-be.necessary₁   IMPFV:PST-COP₂   then

IUs 18-21: 'Revolts rose in our Tibetan area, and he had to go to those (places where the revolts rose)'

IU19 starts with a verb kə-rwês=tə 'NMZL-rise=TOP', which actually forms a clause with IU18. Meanwhile, the final NP in IU19 wəti=ɲeɲê=tə 'there=PL=TOP' is an adjunct to the clause in IU21. However, as the present study restricts the domain of coding to single IUs, an IU like IU19 would be coded as a disjoint IU, without considering the grammatical function its component elements may have when the other IUs were put into consideration.

Criterion ⑥: Truncated, incomplete IUs are not coded for structural types.

4.3. Structural Types of the IU

This subsection provides a sketch of all the structural types observed in the IUs examined for grammatical coding. The structural types are broken down into two major groups: non-clausal and clausal. The remainder of this subsection will start with the non-clausal types, then look into the subtypes of clausal IUs.

4.3.1. Non-Clausal IUs

4.3.1.1. Nominal IUs

Nominal IUs constitute bare nouns (including demonstratives) (144), nouns with a possessive prefix and/or plural or dual suffixes (144), nouns modified by relative clauses (i.e., headed relative clauses) (146), as well as nouns with other non-verbal elements (147).

(144) Bare noun

Narrative14

→ 5. (0.5) {ɐmtsʰo=}
ɐmtsʰô
Amtsho(PN)

6.　toraw ti tə
　　　to-râ-w=ti=tə
　　　PV-find₂-TR=SUB=TOP

IUs 5-6: 'When Amtsho got (the disease)'

(145)　Noun in possessive construction

Narrative01

→　12.　(0.3) {tətʃi wuŋguj} {tʃibjoɲe tə}
　　　　tə-tʃi　　　wə-ŋgu=j　　　　　tʃibjo=ɲê=tə
　　　　N-water　　3SG:POS-inside=LOC　fish=PL=TOP

13.　{katʃop ɐnɐŋorə}
　　　ka-tʃop　　　　　　　ɐ-nɐ-ŋôs=rə
　　　NMZL:PASS-burn₁　　　IRR-PV-COP₂=SUB

IUs 12-13: 'If in the water the fish are burnt'

(146)　NP with a relative clause

Narrative03

174.　{ji^zɐɲe ndzok} {{kərkən wuʒɐk} ti}
　　　jə-zê=ɲê　　　　　　ndzok　kə-rkân　　　　　　wə-ʒɐk=ti
　　　1PL:POS-food=PL　slightly　NMZL-be.short.of₁　3SG:POS-time=
　　　　　　　　　　　　　　　　　　　　　　　　　　　　　TOP:OBL

'At the time when we were a little short of food'

(147) NP and other non-verbal elements

Narrative18

140. (0.5) {təsni ^ti= prerə}
    tə-snî=ti   ptʂêrə
    N-day=TOP:OBL   then

'Then one day'

4.3.1.2. Discourse Markers

In this study, words and phrases are annotated as discourse markers when they are used to structure the discourse without changing its semantic content. Following are the three subtypes of discourse markers coded for Cogtse IUs.

4.3.1.2.1. Connectives

IUs that are constituted by the sequentializer *ptʂê/ptʂ êrə/wuptʂêrə/prë/prêrə* 'then' or the conjunction *korə* 'but, however' are coded as connective IUs, as their primary function is to link parts of discourse. Consider IU14 in example (148).

(148) Narrative02

13. (0.8) wutə mənaŋo {ʃikʰa} {tətə} {kejʒgi}
    wəti= mənaŋorə   ʃikʰa   tətə̂   ke-j-ʒgî
    there= TOP   woods fertilizer NMZL:PL-go.and-find.
                                         and.bring.back₁

'Find fertilizer there in the woods and bring it back'

→ 14. (1.0) ptʂerə=
        ptʂêrə
        then

'Then'

15. (0.6) {kepkor} {kapet}
        ke-pkôr   ka-pêt
        NMZL:PL-carry.on.back$_1$ NMZL:PL-bring.back$_1$

'Carry it on the back and bring it back'

4.3.1.2.2. Pause Fillers

This category includes demonstratives *ʃtə* 'this', *wətə=tə* 'that=TOP', and vocal sounds including *e*, *ẽ*, *ɔ̃*, and *m*. The following example shows two consecutive IUs each of which comprises one pause filler. One of them is a vocal sound (IU13), and the other is a demonstrative (IU14).

(149) Narrative14

   12. (0.6) {ptʂerə}
           ptʂêrə
           then

→ 13. m/
      m
      FIL

→ 14. {wutə tə}
      wətə=tə
      FIL(that=TOP)

15. {ptʂerə} {^smon ndzok tozaŋ wuŋkʰu}
      ptʂêrə   smôn   ndzok   to-za-ŋ=wəŋkʰu
      then   medicine   some   PV-eat$_2$-1SG=after

IUs 12-15: 'Then, mm, well, after I ate some medicine'

4.3.1.2.3. Other Discourse Markers

Other discourse markers in Cogtse include some reactive tokens such as *wâ* 'yes' and attention appealing *o* 'oh'. In example (150) below, the discourse marker *wuʒiŋ* serves to let the listener know that what is coming up in the narrative is something dramatic and exciting.

(150) Narrative08

66. (0.4) {ɲɐ^ndzuj nakəskʰet}
      ɲɐ-ndzûj   na-kə-skʰêt-ɲ
      3PL-fang   PV-PL-take.out$_2$-PL

'(The other people) bared their fangs'

→ 67. (0.7) wuʒiŋ
　　 wuʒiŋ
　　 DM

68. (0.2) {kəsaza kəsamo} {srənmo} {kəpsok}
　　　 {nəŋakpɐn}

kə-saza	kə-samo	srənmô	kə-psok	nə-ŋakpên
NMZL-be,cannibalistic₁	NMZL-be.fierce₁	monster	NMZL-be.like₁	PV-become₂

IUs 67-68: '(They) became (something) like cannibalistic and fierce monsters'

4.3.1.3. Adverbials

Adverbials in Cogtse are lexical words that are used to modify verbs, adjectival verbs or whole clauses. Semantically, they express meanings including location, direction, manner, time, and degree. Morphologically, they do not carry any nominal or verbal inflectional markings; nor do they have unique phonological patterns as ideophones do (cf. §4.3.1.4 for the phonological and morphological characteristics of Cogtse ideophones). The adverbial in example (151) below denotes time.

(151) Narrative08

→ 26. {tʃopon tə}
　　　tʃopon=tə
　　　now=TOP

27. (0.4) {no na^ma te mdɐk}/
　　　no　　na-ma　　　　　te　　mdɐk
　　　2SG　2SG:POS-work　one　be.time.to(do.sth)₁

IUs 26-27: 'Now, it's time (to do) your work'

Some nouns including *sôsni* 'tomorrow', *ndomôr* 'last year' and *tʰɐm* 'nowadays' are used as adverbials in many cases. However, since these words can carry nominal inflection, they are regarded as intrinsically nominal. IUs consisting solely of one of these nouns are therefore coded as nominal IUs. Example (152) below illustrates a case in which *tʰɐm* 'nowadays' serves as a possessor in a possessive construction.

(152) Narrative04

→ 196. (0.6) {^tʰɐm wapuɲe təmənaŋo}
　　　　tʰɐm　　　　　wa-pu=ɲê=təmənaŋorə
　　　　nowadays　　3SG:POS-child=PL=TOP

197. {ɐlɐmɘmə=t}/

ɐlɐmɘmət

IDE:be.brought.up.in.clover

IUs 196-197: 'Children of nowadays are brought up in clover'

4.3.1.4. Ideophone

An ideophone is a representation of events that can be experienced by senses i.e., 'the manner how an event is heard, seen, touched, smelled and felt psychologically' (Kilian-Hatz 2001: 157). By a large consensus in the literature, ideophones function to simulate via language an event with emotion and perception (Voeltz & Kilian-Hatz 2001: 2). As has already been observed by Doke, ideophones are not always onomatopoeic, but they are distinguished from other words by special phonological traits (in Voeltz and Kilian-Hatz (2001: 1)). They are 'simplexes' in form, without markings for person, tense and mood for verbs, or those for case, number and gender for nouns (Kilian-Hatz 2001: 156). Cogtse ideophones reveal many of the prototypical characteristics of ideophones observed in African languages. [3] In morphological terms, although Cogtse ideophones are similar to adverbials in that they do not carry

---

3   J. Sun and Shih (2004)give a detailed description of ideophones in the Caodeng dialect and posit them as a distinct lexical category on account of their unique phonological, morphological, and syntactic characteristics.

any verbal or nominal inflection, they do have a phonological trait that sets them apart from other lexical categories in the language. That is, they do not contrast /HL/ and /∅/, and are always on Melody 2 of /∅/ (cf. §2.3.2 for detailed discussion on Melody 2 of /∅/), as illustrated in examples (153) and (154).

(153) *bojboj* [H-L] 'choppy, fleshy, very cute, with rosy complexion, rather introverted (in the good sense)'

(154) *ɟrɐpɟrɐp* [H-L] 'very fat, but the muscle is rather loose, with the belly so huge that you can shake it'

As is also shown in the above examples, ideophones almost always occur in reduplicated form, which in general is not a very common and productive word-formation process in Cogtsc.

Example (155) below shows a case in which an ideophone *zizik* is used to modify the verb *na-kə-ɲi-s* 'IMPFV: PST-NMZL-sit-PST'.

(155) Narrative08

47. (0.2) {lɐmɐ te} {wuksə te} {{zi=kzik naŋɲis} nəŋo}

lɐmê te	wətə-kəsə̂n	te	**zikzik**	na-kə-ɲi-s	nə-ŋos
lama one	that-way	one	**IDE:upright**	IMPFV:PST-NMZL-sit$_2$-PST	OBV-COP1

'A lama was sitting that way, upright (in there)'

Ideophones can occur in isolation, constituting single IUs by themselves, as demonstrated in examples (156) and (157).

(156) Narrative04

196. (0.6) {^tʰɐm wapuɲe təmənaŋo}
tʰɐ̂m   wa-pu=ɲê=təmənaŋorə
nowadays   3SG:POS-child=PL=TOP

→ 197. {ɐlɐməmə=t}/
ɐlɐməmət
IDE:be.brought.up.in.clover

IUs 196-197: 'Children of nowadays are brought up in clover'

(157) Narrative12

20. korə {wətə} wə-
korə   wətə   wə-
but   that   3SG:POS-

21. {kʰɐkpəɲe wɐskrən tə} {ahwaŋ}
kʰɐkpə̂=ɲê   wɐ-skrə̂n=tə   ahwaŋ
story=PL   3SG:POS-be.long=TOP   Afang(PN)

→ 22. (0.5) {pʰɐ^lɐpʰɐrtsʰəm}
pʰɐlɐpʰɐrtsʰəm
IDE:fragmentary

23. {te ^ŋo wuŋkʰu} {makanəncʰa} {wo}

te	ŋôs=wəŋkʰu	ma-ka-nəncʰa	wô
one	COP=SUB	NEG-NMZL:PL-be.capable₁	PART

IUs 20-23: 'The story is so very long, Afang, fragmentary, can't do it'

4.3.1.5. Onomatopoetics

Onomatopoetic expressions alone are also observed to constitute independent IUs. Example (158) shows an onomatopoetic IU that simulates the sound of dog barking.

(158) Narrative19

73. {kʰowuŋ} {{stoŋ kəsna} təməna}

kʰowuŋ	stoŋ	kə-sna=təmənaŋorə
Tibetan.mastiff	the.most	NMZL-be.good₁=TOP

→ 74. (0.4) {hoŋ}
hoŋ
ONM

75. (0.5) {hoŋ ^hoŋ kətsə tə}
    hoŋhoŋ   kə-tsə̂s=tə
    ONOM   NMZL-say₁=TOP

IUs 73-75: "'The best Tibetan mastiffs bark like 'hong, hong hong'" he said'

4.3.2. Clausal IUs

In Cogtse, except for very few cases of verb-less clauses (cf. § 4.3.2.1.3), every clause has a verbal predicate as its core. The number of clause(s) enclosed in an IU is equal to the number of verbal predicate(s) in it. Clausal IUs can be either mono-clausal or multi-clausal. This subsection will present the subtypes of clausal IUs and their constructions.

4.3.2.1. Mono-Clausal IUs

A mono-clausal IU consists of one single clause, which can be either finite or non-finite. I further distinguish between two types of finite clauses: fully finite clauses and nominalized finite clauses, depending on whether the verbal predicate is nominalized.

4.3.2.1.1. Fully Finite Clauses

A fully finite clause has a verb that carries the finite verbal inflection of the clause. The verb is not nominalized, and can carry a full range of inflectional markers to denote information about tense, aspect, modality (henceforth TAM), person, and number. In example (159) below, IU18 consists of a finite clause, the verb of which (*nɐ-ɲi-ŋ* 'PFV-live-1SG') inflects for perfectivity and a first-person singular S.

(159) Narrative07

16. {{mdorʥe wuʒimkʰam} mənaŋorə=}/
     mdorʥet   wə-ʒimkʰâm=mənaŋorə
     Long'erjia(PLN)   3SG:POS-area=TOP

17. {ʃtʃenəs pa=}
     ʃtʃenə̂s-pa
     twelve-year

→ 18. {{{wuro cem} te} nɐɲi=ŋ}/
     wə-ro   cem   te   nɐ-ɲi-ŋ
     3SG:POS-surplus   more.or.less one   PFV-live₂-1SG

IUs 16-18: 'I lived at the Long'erjia area for about twelve years'

4.3.2.1.2. Nominalized Finite Clauses

A nominalized finite clause can make up an independent IU in Cogtse.[4] Such IUs consist of a nominalized verb that also

---

4 For an overview and case studies of nominalization in Tibeto-Burman languages, see Genetti et al. 2008.

carries inflection of TAM (but not evidentiality), person, and number. While the whole array of perfective prefixes is retained in this structure, the several imperfective subtypes collapse into a single zero-marked general imperfective in contrast with the perfective. In other words, the verb in the nominalized finite clause shows reduced finiteness. Example (160) demonstrates a nominalized imperfective clause in IU120.

(160) Narrative18

119. (0.5) {[wɐkɐj ti] mənaŋo} {wumo} w- sə-
     wɐkɐ̂j=ti=mənaŋorə   wə-mô
     originally=TOP:OBL=TOP   3SG:POS-mother

→ 120. (0.9) wuwɐj rə {məkəsnas}
     wəwɐ̂j=rə   mə-kə-snâ-s
     to.her=TOP   NEG:IMPFV:PST-NMZL-be.good$_2$-PST

IUs 119-120: 'Originally he was not kind to his mother'

Although the present study is in principle "minimalistic", it scrutinizes the various functions the nominalized finite clause has when adjacent IUs are considered. It has been revealed that this grammatical structureis used to serve a number of distinct grammatical functions.

Based on the data examined, with adjacent IUs nominalized finite clauses in Cogtse can function as follows:

adverbial clauses, relative clauses, complement clauses, or medial clauses in a clause chain. As already shown in §4.2, nominalized finite clauses in the same structural formulation (nominalized finite clause + =*ti*) can serve either as an adverbial clause or a relative clause. In the two examples provided in §4.2, repeated here in (161) and (162) for convenience, the two nominalized finite clauses both end with an oblique topicalizer =*ti*.

(161) Nominalized finite clause= relative clause

Narrative08

→ 6. (0.5) {didi kə} {kəjam=ti}
     didî=kə   kə-jâm=ti
     gradually=INST NMZL-be.wide₁=TOP:OBL

'(The place where the road) is wider and wider'

7. (0.5) {<x> sə^stoŋ ti nəkəkʃut nəŋo}
    sʊstôŋ=ti   nə-kə-kʃût   nə-ŋos
    wasteland=TOP:OBL   PFV-NMZL-come.out₂   OBV-COP₁

'(He) came out to a wasteland'

(162) Nominalized finite clause= adverbial clause

Narrative18

→ 152. (0.5) {kəjam kəstsə^stsə= ti ptʂe}

kəjam	kə-stsəstsə̂=ti		ptʂe
sun	NMZL-be.hot$_1$:REDU=TOP:OBL		then

153. {təmu ^rəwɟir napu ptʂe}

tə-mû	rə̂w-ɟir	nâ-pʉ-w	ptʂê
N-weather	as.soon.as/right.away-change	PFV:EVI-do$_1$-TR	then

IUs 152-153: 'While it was sunny and hot, the weather suddenly changed'

Another related example is provided in (163). In this case, the nominalized finite clause (IU73) is marked with a regular topicalizer =tə, and it is interpreted as a headless relative clause when the following IU (IU 74) is considered.

(163) Narrative20

→ 73. {{ŋəmi kətsam} tə}/

ŋə-mi	kə-tsâm=tə
1SG:POS-daughter	NMZL-take.away=TOP

74. {kəsce} {tə^tʃi nəkpiɲe nɐjkəŋo}/

kə-scê	tə-tʃî	nə-kə-pi=ɲê	nɐ̂j-kə-ŋos
NMZL-be.preceding	N-water	PFV:west-NMZL-come$_2$=PL	IMPFV:PST:EVI-PL-COP$_1$

IUs 73-74: 'What took my daughter away was the water

that came here earlier (lit. the earlier water that came here)'

Nominalized finite clauses that serve as complement clauses are rare (only 5 tokens out of 510 nominalized finite clauses). Example (164) below shows in IU5 a complement clause in the form of a nominalized finite clause (IU5).[5] (Note that the same combination of [NOMINALIZED FINITE CLAUSE + =tə] in IU6 must be interpreted as a relative clause.)

(164) Narrative03

    3. {ŋɐpɐ=}
       ŋɐ-pê
       1SG:POS-father

    4. (1.1) e=
       e
       FIL

    5. {tʰe^ɲe nɐkpu tə=}
       tʰe=ɲê   nɐ-kə-pê-w=tə
       what=PL   PFV?-NMZ-do$_2$-TR=TOP

IUs 3-5: 'Then, what my father did'

---

5 An alternative analysis of IU5 simply treats the nominalized finite clause as a topic, which has no direct grammatical relation with the verb *tsə̂s-ŋ* '(say$_1$-1SG)' in IU6.

6. {ŋa} {kəʃiŋ tə} {teɲe} {tsəŋ}

ŋa	kə-ʃî-ŋ=tə	te=ɲê	tsâs-ŋ
1SG	NMZ-know₁-1SG=TOP	one=PL	say₁-1SG

'I will talk about what I know'

In the twenty narratives that are examined for the present study, the nominalized finite clause is used most frequently in clause chains. This clause-linking strategy is never discussed in previous literature on the Rgyalrong language, and can only be observed in non-elicited discourse data.(; ; ;) (; ; ;)A Cogtse clause chain comprises two or more clauses, the last of which is fully finite (i.e., carries full inflection without a nominalizer), while the other clauses are partially finite and marked with a nominalizer on the verb. The medial clauses do not serve as arguments of the final clause, nor is there any specific morphological marking that indicate any adverbial relation. The clauses in a clause chain represent coherent (but not necessarily temporally sequential) ideas in a sequence as shown in example (165) below. Note that the final clause (IU20) is fully finite, while the medial clause (IU17) is nominalized with kə- and shows reduced finiteness (with no evidential marking, compared with the verb in IU20).

(165) Narrative08

→ 17. (0.6) {{wujo rə} wuʒi} {ɲapsoˆsoj naŋnis ptʂe}

    wəjol=rə=wuʒi   ɲa-psopsô=j   na-kə-ɲi-s

    3SG:POS=TOP=PART   3PL:POS(monks)-side=LOC   **PFV-NMZL-sit₂-PST**

'He sat next to them (i.e., the lamas in the temple)'

18. (0.4) {wutʂə} na-
    wə-tʂi
    3SG:POS-front

19. (0.4) {{wutə tʰamtʃɐ} wurmi} {nəkəntʃʰɐr tə}
    wətə   stʰamtʃɐ̂t   wə-rmî   nə-kə-ntʃʰɐr=tə
    that   all   3SG:POS-person   PFV-NMZL-appear=TOP

→ 20. {lɐˆndʐə naŋakpɐn} {lu}
    lɐndʐə̂   **nâ-ŋakpɐn**   lu
    ghost   **PFV:EVI-become**   PART

IUs 18-20: 'All the people that had appeared in front of him became ghosts'

The Cogtse clause chain is crucially distinct from converb constructions in that the latter must have non-finite medial verbs (Bickel 1998; Genetti 2005; Haspelmath 1995), while

Cogtse medial clauses are always (partially) finite.[6] Note that there are two nominalizers that can be used in the Cogtse clause chain: *kə-* and *ka-*. The nominalizer *ka-* is applied when one of the arguments is human and non-singular (i.e., plural or dual), while *kə-* is used elsewhere. Example (166) shows an imperfective medial clause (IU46). Here the nominalizer *kə-* is used because the subject is a body part (i.e., the esophagus). The medial clause (IU46) describes a general situation, while the final clause (IU47) provides a specific instance of that situation.

(166) Narrative14

46. (0.6) ko {wɐtʃɐtʃɐj} {kərɐk}

korə	wɐtʃɐtʃɐpj	**kə-rɐ̂k**
but	sometimes	**NMZL-get.stuck**

47. {jaɲju wuŋkʰu} {kʰɐlɐk} {wtə morə} {{kasi mənakʰut} wuji}/

jaɲju=wəŋkʰu	kʰɐlɐk	wətə=morə
potato=after/and	tsamba.lump	that=PART
ka-sə-jî		mə-na-kʰut=wuji
NMZL-CAUS-go.down		NEG-OBV-be.allowed=PART

---

6 In Genetti et al. (2008: 124), I analyzed the medial clauses of a clause chain as non-finite. In light of more profound and detailed examination of a larger dataset, I would revise the analysis and mark all medial clauses in the Cogtse clause chain as (partially) finite. Nominalized verbs that constitute medial clauses denote imperfectivity if they do not bear any tense-aspect prefix.

IUs 46-47: 'But sometimes it (esophagus) gets stuck, it is impossible to swallow potatoes and tsamba lumps (lit. letting potatoes and tsamba lumps go down is not allowed)'

In example (167), the verb in the medial clause (IU50) is nominalized with *ka-* to index the agent, which is human and dual (i.e., non-singular). Again, in this example, the medial and final clauses do not have shared arguments.

(167) Narrative11

50. ptʂerə {{sɐgɐs te} nɐkɐpɐ} {^ptʂe maŋkʰridʒe}

ptʂêrə	sɐgɐs1	te	nɐ-kɐ-pề		ptʂêrə	maŋkʰri11=ndʒes
then	party	one	PFV-**NMZL:PL**-do$_2$		then	pitiful=DU

51. {tə^cʰas [kəcʰantʃ] jiktʰɐntʃ nəŋo ptʂerə}

təcʰas	jə-kə-tʰɐl-ntʃ		nə-ŋos	ptʂêrə
together	PFV-NMZL-go$_2$-2/3DU		OBV-COP$_1$	then

IUs 50-51: 'Then (the rich ones) gave a party, and the two pitiful ones went together (to the party)'

Table 4.4 summarizes the distribution of the functions the
nominalized finite clause serves:

	Medial clauses in the clause chain	Adverbial clauses	Relative clauses	Complement clauses	Total
Number of IUs	371	66	68	5	510
Percentage	73%	13%	13%	1%	100%

Table 4.4 Functions of the nominalized finite clause with adjacent IUs

As shown in this table, there is a salient disparity in frequency
between clause-chaining and the other functions. Out of the 510
IUs coded as nominalized finite clauses, there are 371 medial
clauses (73%), 68 relative clauses (13%), 66 adverbial clauses
(13%), and only 5 complement clauses (1%).

4.3.2.1.3. Non-Finite Clauses

A non-finite clause consists of a verb stem prefixed with
the infinitive nominalizer *ka-/kɐ-*. In the narratives examined,
all the non-finite clausal IUs end with a general topicalizer, and
they are used to refer to a topic in discourse. Example (168)
starts with a non-finite clausal IU ending with a topicalizer
=mənaŋorə (IU45), and all the IUs that follow it are about the
topic that IU45 refers to.

(168) Narrative02

→ 45. (1.9) {{təjeŋkʰu kapa} mənaŋorə}

tə-jeŋkʰu	ka-pa=mənaŋorə
N-farm.field.flattening	NMZL-do_1=TOP

'As for flattening the farm field'

46. (0.7) ẽ=/

ẽ
FIL

47. (0.4) {tɐjɐkkorti tə=}/

tɐ-jɐkkortî=tə
N-handy.tool=TOP

IUs 46-47: 'As for the handy tools'

48. (0.5) {{{kɐk kɐdʐ̩ət} ʒi} kʰu=t}/

kɐ̂k	kɐ-dʐ̩ə̂t=ʒi	kʰut
hoe	NMZL-$take_2$=also	$be.allowed_1$

'Taking a hoe will do'

49. (0.8) ptʂ̩erə

ptʂ̩êrə
then

50. {pʰu^ɟɐ kɐdzət ʒi kʰu=t}/

pʰuɟê	kɐ-dzə̂t=ʒi	kʰut
(tool.to.smash.soil.blocks)	NMZL-take₁=also	be.allowed₁

IUs 49-50: 'Taking the tool that smashes soil blocks will do'

51. (1.2) ptʂerə

ptʂêrə

then

52. (1.8) {{təʃlo kɐlɐt} ti}

tə-ʃlo	kɐ-lêt=ti
N-turning.over.the.soil	NMZL:PL-put[1]=TOP:OBL

53. {{{pʰu tokəkʃut}ɲet} mənaŋorə}

pʰu	to-kə-kʃût=ɲê=təmənaŋorə
soil.block	PFV-NMZL-come/go.out₂=PL=TOP

54. (0.7) {wətə tə=}

wətə=tə

that=TOP

55. (0.4) {kastsu=}

ka-stsû

NOM:PL-smash₁

IUs 51-55: 'then, we smash the soil blocks that come out when we turn over the soil'

56. (0.3) {wuɟələkɲe} {kantu=}

wə-ɟəlǝk=ɲê	ka-ntû
3SG:POS-rock=PL	NMZL:PL-pick.up₁

'We pick up the rocks (in the soil)'

57. ptşe {ʃtə təmǝnaŋorǝ} {təje kɐlɐt ŋo=s}/

ptşê	ʃtə= təmǝnaŋorǝ	tə-je	kɐ-lêt	ŋôs
then	this= TOP	N-sowing	NMZL-release₁	COP₁

'And this is sowing'

Cogtse has verbless clauses, but their occurrences are very rare in the dataset (only two tokens). They are therefore treated as non-finite copular clauses for analytical convenience. Example (169) illustrates one of the verb-less clauses observed in the narratives (IU63).

(169) Narrative07

62. {{mbro kɐdzət} na^ra=s ptşe} {wujoɲe=}

mbro	kɐ-dzə̂t	na-râ-s	ptşê	wəjoɲê
horse	NMZL-take₁	IMPFV:PST-be.necessary₂-PST	then	3PL

→ 63. {ɲi^mbro tə} {kəsa=m}

    ɲə-mbro=tə   kəsâm

    3PL:POS-horse=TOP   three

IUs 62-63: 'it was necessary to take horses along, and they had three horses (literally: their horses were three)'

64. {wutətə} {waʃnoɲe naka^ta pre}

    wətə=tə   wa-ʃno=ɲê   na-ka-tâ   ptşê

    that=TOP   3SG:POS-saddle=PL PFV-NMZL:PASS-put$_2$ then

'They (the horses) are saddled up (literally: their saddles have been put on)'

4.3.2.1.4. Relative Clauses

Cogtse relative clauses can be either finite or non-finite, but they all have to be nominalized. Head-external relative clauses are linked to the head noun in the main clause by a third-person singular possessive prefix wə-. Consider example (170). The relative clause is enclosed in square brackets, and the third-person singular possessive prefix is printed in bold.

(170) Narrative05

22. (1.3) {njaŋ^şan kɐtsə wuʒimkʰam ti mənaŋorə}

    [njaŋşan   kɐ-tsâs]   **wə**-ʒimkʰâm=ti=mənaŋorə

    Liangshan(PLN)   NMZL:GP-say$_1$ **3SG:POS**-area=TOP:OBL=TOP

'At the area called Liangshan'

Non-finite relative clauses are formed out of participant deverbal nouns carrying nominalzing prefixes that signify the grammatical role of the deverbal noun: *kə-* (for S/A arguments), *ka-/kɐ-* (for P argument) and *sa-/sɐ* (for obliques). If the relative verb is transitive, the non-finite relative clause can also take a possessive prefix that represents one of the core arguments S/A or P.[7] Consider example (171). IU140 contains a headless, non-finite relative clause *wə-ka-nərga* '3SG:POS-NMZL:PAT-like'. The relative verb carries the nominalizer *ka-*, which signifies that the relative NP is a P argument. Meanwhile, the nominalized verb is prefixed with a possessive marker to indicate that the A argument of the relative verb is third person singular.

(171) Narrative03

139. (0.5) {wutə tə=}
        wətə=tə
        that=TOP

---

7 For a more detailed description of relative clauses in Cogtse, readers may refer to Wei (2001). For a cross-dialectal analysis of Rgyalrong relativization, cf. J. Sun and Y. Lin (2007).

→ 140. (0.6) e {wuka^nərga naŋo ptʂerə}

    e   [wə-ka-nərga]   na-ŋôs   ptʂêrə

    PART   3SG:POS-NMZL:PAT-like₁   IMPFV:PST-COP₂ then

IUs 139-140: 'This was what he liked'

Finite relative clauses are all nominalized with *kə-*, and carry finite inflection for person, number, and tense-aspect. Like the nominalized finite clauses introduced in §4.3.2.1.2, finite relative clauses do not distinguish the various subtypes of imperfectives. General imperfectivity is denoted by zeromarking in contrast with the perfective form.

In the present study, IUs constituted of headed relative clauses are coded as nominal IUs (cf. §4.3.1.1). Only IUs that are constituted of headless relative clause(s) are coded as relative-clause IUs. This IU type is distinct from the type of nominalized finite clause in that its nominalized verb must carry some nominal inflectional markers, such as an ergative case marker or nominal dual and plural enclitics. With these markers, one can determine a relative-clause IU without considering any adjacent IUs.

Consider the relative-clause IU in example (172) below. IU21 comprises an imperfective, headless relative clause that is modified by an adverbial *ndzok* 'slightly'. The whole clause is then followed by a nominal dual marker that indicates the number of the relative NP. In fact, IU25 further confirms that IU21 is a headless relative clause. However, one can actually determine the structural type of IU21 only by examining the morphosyntactic taxonomy of the IU in question.

(172) Narrative15

→ 21. {ndzok} {{kənəwɐrjondʒe} tə} {ptʂerə}
    [ndzok   kə-nəwɐtjô]=ndʒês=tə   ptʂêrə
    slightly   NMZL-be,hardworking₁=DU=TOP then

    22. m
       m
       FIL

    23. {ptʂerə}
       ptʂêrə
       then

    24. {^ndzok ana=}
       ndzok   ana
       slightly FIL

    25. {dʒɐspɐ [dzɐspɐ] } {{nəŋmaʃentsə} nəŋo}/
       dʒɐspê   nə-kə-maʃe-ntʃ   nə-ŋos
       quite   PFV-NMZL-be.rich₂-2/3DU OBV-COP₁

IUs 21-25: 'The two hardworking ones then became rather rich'

4.3.2.1.5. Adverbial Clauses

Like relative-clause IUs (§4.3.2.1.4), an adverbial-clause IU must bear some morphosyntactic marking that can make one determine its structural type without considering adjacent IUs. In Cogtse, a temporal adverbial subordinate clause carries an enclitic which denotes the semantic relationship of the adverbial clause to the following clause. The most common subordinators observed in the database are *=ti* 'when' and *=wuŋkʰuj* 'after'. Example (173) below shows an adverbial clause with *=ti* 'when', while Example (174) demonstrates an adverbial clause with *=wuŋkʰuj* 'after'.

(173) Narrative20

50. {tʃimtoj namdu [namdə] ti[tə]} {prerə}
    tʃimto=j   na-mdu=ti   ptʂêrə
    riverside=LOC   PFV:down-arrive₂=when   then

'When he arrived at the riverside'

(174) Narrative11

→ 98. {toŋasatsa wuŋkʰuj}

   to-ŋa-sastâ=wəŋkʰuj

   PFV-MID-place₂=after

99. ptʂɐr wapuɲe [tapundʒe] zur {kə^wdi= nakasəɲi nəŋo}

  {tapu kəwdi}

ptʂê	wa-pu=ɲê	zur	kəwdî	nâ
then	3SG:POS-child=PL	corner	four	downwards
na-ka-sə-ɲi		nə-ŋos	ta-pu	kəwdî
PFV-NMZL:PASS-CAUS-sit₂		OBV-COP₁	N-child	four

IUs 98-99: 'After (the food) was placed (on the table), then the four children were seated at the four corners of the table'

Conditional adverbial clauses, on the other hand, are formed from special conditional verb forms and their associated core arguments.[8] For example, the conditional verb form in IU109 of (175) is formed with a verb stem2 prefixed by the conditional prefix *mə-* and a perfective prefix *na-*, and followed by a subordinating enclitic =*rə*.

(175) Narrative06

---

8   Cf. Y. Lin (2000) for the formation of Cogtse conditional verb forms.

→ 109. {{karmagam mənasamto} rə=}

karmâ-gam   mə-na-samtô=rə
eared.pheasant-egg   COND-PFV-be.seen₂=SUB

110. {{tɐŋgoj te} kɐcʰop}

tɐŋgoj   te   kɐ-cʰôp
in.the.first.place one   NMZL:GP-smash₁

IUs 109-110: 'If an eared-pheasant egg was seen, (we) would smash one in the first place'

4.3.2.2. Multi-Clausal IUs

Multi-clausal IUs are IUs that consist of more than one clause. These are additionally sub-classified depending on the ways the clauses are combined.

4.3.2.2.1. Complex Sentences

In the present study, complex sentences are defined as sentences comprising one subordinate clause and one main clause. Complex sentences that contain any number of multi-clausal sentences are identified as "super-complex", and will be discussed in §4.3.2.2.4. The reason for this decision is pragmatic, as it would be very difficult to analyze and calculate the distribution of different types of subordinate clauses if the super-complex IUs were included. Following are examples of complex sentences formed respectively with a complement clause (176) , a relative clause (177), and an adverbial clause (178). The subordinate clauses are enclosed in square brackets.

(176) Complex sentence: complement clause + main clause

Narrative06

67. {tṣo^zon kɐnəndz̩ət ^ra= ptṣerə}

[tṣozôn	kɐ-nə-ndz̩ət]	râ	ptṣêrə
travel.food	NMZL-each-take$_1$	be.necessary$_1$	then

'It was necessary (for each of us) to take travel food along'

(177) Complex sentence: relative clause + main clause

Narrative11

131. {stoŋ} {kəra tə} {tə^rmi nəŋo ptṣe}

[stôŋ	kə-râ]=tə		tə-rmî	nə-ŋos	ptṣê
the.most	NMZL-be.necessary$_1$=TOP		N-person	OBV-COP$_1$	then

'The most necessary (thing) is people'

(178) Complex sentence: adverbial clause + main clause

Narrative07

11. {maŋmə} {kəwdəpa} {nɐ^pɐ=ŋ wuŋkʰuj ptṣerə}
    {jinəja=ŋ}

[maŋmɔ̂	kəwdɔ̂-pa	nɐ-pɐ̂-ŋ=wəŋkʰuj]	ptṣêrə	jə-nəjâ-ŋ
militia	four-year	PFV-do$_2$-1SG=after	then	PFV-go/come.home$_2$-1SG

'After serving in the army for four years, I came home'

4.3.2.2.2. Sequential Sentences

In a sequential sentence, clauses are linked by a sequentializer. In the Cogtse narratives examined, several IUs consist of two or more clauses that are linked to each other by *tṣêrə*/prêrə/ *ptṣê/prê* 'then'. For example:

(179) Narrative20

15. (0.8) {tətʃi kə} {jatsam} {pre} {ɹɐlpo rə} {tənəsu^su=
wji}

tə-tʃi=kə	jâ-tsam	ptṣê	ɹɐlpô=rə	tə-nəsusu	wuji
N-water=ERG	PFV:EVI-take.away₁	then	king=TOP	N-be.sad₁	DM

'The water took away (the king's daughter), and the king was very very sad'

4.3.2.2.3. Juxtaposed Clauses

In the database, there are a number of multi-clausal IUs in which clauses are combined via juxtaposition, without any intervening linkers in between or grammatical markers that signify embedding, consecutivization, or coordination. For example:

(180) Narrative14

61. tʰe nəpapaw tʃokpon {^sannjɐn cem ʒi tso}/

tʰe	nə-papa-w	tʃokpon		
what	each-do$_1$-TR	now		
sánnjɐn		cem=ʒi		tso
three.years(Chinese.loan)		more.or.less=already		elapse$_1$

'Whatever happens, three years have elapsed'

Note that the cohesion between the two clauses in (180)-- *tʰe nə-papa-w* 'whatever happens' and *sánnjɐn cem=ʒi tso* 'it has been three years-- is signified via nothing but juxtaposition. No intervening grammatical markers are used to show the semantic relation between these two clauses.

Consider another example of an IU of juxtaposed clauses in (181). Here again the two clauses-- *kam na-ŋa-tu* 'the door was open' and *wa-tʂʰo ko-nəmcɐrɐ-ŋ=ko* 'I saw the light' are combined via nothing but juxtaposition.

(181) Narrative08

87. (0.1) {kam naŋatu} {{watʂʰo konəmcɐrɐŋ} ko}

kam	na-ŋa-tu	watʂʰo	ko-nəmcɐrɐ-ŋ=ko
door	OBV-INTR[9]-open$_1$	3SG:POS-light	IMPFV:SP-look.at$_2$-1SG=DM

---

9 For a detailed discussion of the intransitivizer *ŋa-*, cf. Wei (2001), especially §4.4.

'The door was open, I saw the light'

The IU of juxtaposed clauses presented below in (182) shows many grammatical and semantic properties that are used to characterize serial-verb constructions in some major cross-linguistic studies (Aikhenvald & Dixon 2006; Bisang 1995; Foley & Olson 1985; Langacker 2003; Li 1991; Lord 1993):

(182) Narrative02

13. (0.8) wutə mənaŋo {ʃikʰa} {tətə} {kɐjʒgi}

wəti= mənaŋorə	ʃikʰa	tətɔ̂	kɐ-j-ʒgî
there= TOP	woods	fertilizer	NMZL:GP-go.and-find.
			and.bring.back₁

'Find fertilizer there in the woods and bring it back'

14. (1.0) ptʂerə=

ptʂêrə

then

'Then'

→ 15. (0.6) {kɐpkor} {kapet}

kɐ-pkôr	ka-pêt
NMZL:GP -carry.on.back₁	NMZL:GP -bring.back₁

'Carry it on the back and bring it back'

First of all, *kɐ-pkôr* and *ka-pêt* make up a sequence of verbs without overt connective morphemes. They have shared arguments and verbal inflection. Semantically, together they denote one event. In other words, the juxtaposed clauses in (182) make a more prototypical serial-verb construction than the juxtaposed clauses in (180) and (181).

4.3.2.2.4. Super-Complex Clausal IUs

Super-complex clausal IUs are those that consist of more than one multi-clausal construction. For example, in (183) below, in addition to an adverbial clause (enclosed in square brackets), the IU also has a headless relative clause *tʰe kə-ndo* 'what NMZL-there.be' functioning as the object to the verbal core of the matrix clause (*kə-pa* 'NMZL-do1'):

(183) Narrative19

16. (0.4) {wa^ro te tozor ti} {^tʰe kədo kəpa}/

[wa-rô	te	to-zor=ti]	tʰe	kə-ndo	kə-pa
3SG:POS-chest	one	PFV-ache$_2$=SUB	what	NMZL-there.be$_1$	NMZL-do$_1$

'When he became angry, he did whatever there was (to do)'

IUs constituted of quotative constructions are usually super-complex constructions. Example (184) below shows a serial-verb construction (enclosed in square brackets) that functions as the object of the matrix verb *to-ka-tsis nə-ŋos* 'PFV-NMZL:PL-say$_2$ OBV-COP$_1$':

(184) Narrative08

129. (0.3) {^sruŋ atotəsk^{h}et} {wu^p^{h}is na ɐnɐtə^lwak tokatsi nəŋo}

[srûŋ	a-to-tə-sk^{h}et	wə-p^{h}î-s	nâ
talisman	IRR-PFV-2-take.out$_1$	3SG:POS-outside-LOC	downwards
ɐ-nɐ-tə-lwâk]		to-ka-tsis	nə-ŋos
IRR-PFV:downwards-2-hang$_1$		PFV-NMZL:PL-say$_2$	OBC-COP$_1$

'"Take out the talisman and hang it down outside (of your clothes)" (the Lama) said'

4.4. Distribution of Structural Types

Of the 3,253 IUs in all the narratives examined, 223 IUs (7%) are truncated and are not considered for structural types. That is to say, 3,030 IUs in the database are analyzed for grammatical coding. The distribution of the major structural types coded in these IUs is presented in Table 4.5.

Unit Types		IU Number	Percentage (of all IUs)
Clausal		**1758**	**58.0%**
	Mono-Clausal	1208	39.9%
	Multi-Clausal	550	18.2%
	Complex Senences	351	11.6%
	w/ Complement CL(s)	273	9.0%
	w/ Relative CL(s)	73	2.4%
	w/ Adverbial CL(s)	5	0.2%
	Super-Complex Sentences	137	4.5%
	Juxtaposed Sentences	48	1.6%
	Sequential Sentences	14	0.5%
Non-Clausal		**1183**	**39.0%**
	Nominal	615	20.3%
	NP	587	19.4%
	NP w/ relative CL	28	0.9%
	Discourse Markers	507	16.7%
	Connectives	241	8.0%
	FIL	229	7.6%
	Other Discourse Markers	37	1.2%
	Others (Adverbials, ideophones, onomatopoetic)	61	2.0%
Disjoint		**89**	**2.9%**
Total		**3030**	**100%**

Table 4.5 Distribution of structural types in Cogtse IUs

The distribution of finite and non-finite clauses is also examined. Multi-clausal IUs are categorized for finiteness by the final verb they contain. The result shows that clausal IUs are predominantly finite (95%). Among the finite clauses, 70%

are fully finite, while 30% are finite verbs prefixed with a nominalizer. Consider Table 4.6 for the distribution.

	IU number	Percentage
Finite Clauses	1675	**95%**
Fully finite	1165	70% (of all finite clauses)
Nominalized finite	510	30% (of all finite clauses)
Non-Finite Clauses	83	**5%**
Total	1758	**100%**

Table 4.6 Distribution of finite and non-finite clauses

4.5. Discussion of the Results

4.5.1. The Preferred Structural Type

In §3.0, it was mentioned that the present study aims to determine the preferred structural type in Cogtse IUs; and later in §4.2, it was demonstrated that the present study follows the "one verb, one clause" guideline as proposed by Tao (1996) and Iwasaki and Tao (1993) in coding clausal IUs in Cogtse.

The overall distribution of structural types presented in 4.4 demonstrates that in this language, clausal intonation units outnumber non-clausal IUs by 58%:39%. The result suggests that Cogtse is more similar to English than to Mandarain Chinese in that the clausal type is dominant in IUs, [10]

---

10 It should be noted, however, in comparison with the proportion of clausal IUs Chafe (1987; 1994) discovered in spontaneous English (60%-70%), the proportion of clausal IUs in spontaneous Cogtse is slightly lower (58%). This

irrespective of the fact that, with its much more complex morphosyntactic structuring, Cogtse is typologically distinct from both Mandarin Chinese and English.[11]

4.5.2. Complex IUs vs. the "One Clause per IU" Tendency

In comparison with related studies in other languages (for example Chafe (1980), Croft (1995)), the proportion of multi-clausal IUs in Cogtse is surprisingly high (39%, as opposed to 19%, 14.2%, or 3% in English as found by Croft (1995), which varies depending on how Croft defines "clause"). Consider Table 4.7 for the distribution of mono-clausal and multi-clausal IUs in Cogtse:

Clausal	1758	100%
Mono-Clausal	1208	69%
Multi-Clausal	550	31%

Table 4.7 Distribution of mono-clausal IUs and multi-Clausal IUs among all clausal IUs

Table 4.8 below gives the distribution of all the subtypes of the multi-clausal IUs. Complex sentences with complement clauses outnumber all the other multi-clausal types, while

---

could mean that IUs correlate to the clause to a lesser degree in Cogtse than in English.

11 Dolakha Newar, another Tibeto-Burman language noted for complex morphosyntactic structuring, is also reported to have more clausal IUs than non-clausal ones in spontaneous speech (Genetti & Slater 2004).

complex sentences with embedded adverbial clauses are the least frequent (only five tokens). Super-complex sentences also appear many times (137 tokens, 25%), more frequently than juxtaposed clauses (9%) and sequential sentences (3%).

	Number	Percentage
Complex Sentences	**351**	**63%**
w/ Complement clauses	273	49%
Quotative Constructions	145	53% (of all complement clauses)
Others	128	47% (of all complement clauses)
w/ Relative Clauses	73	13%
w/ Adverbial Clauses	5	1%
Super-complex Sentences	**137**	**25%**
Juxtaposed Clauses	**48**	**9%**
Sequential Sentences	**14**	**3%**
Total	**557**	**100%**

Table 4.8 Distribution of the subtypes of multi-clausal IUs

As reviewed in §3.0, it has been proposed that ideally the upper limit to the grammatical size of an IU is a single clause, grounded on considerations regarding cognitive information processing (Chafe 1980; 1994; 1996; 1998; Halliday 1967; 1985). The present subsection therefore explores possible factors that could account for such a high proportion of Cogtse IUs that do not follow the "one clause per IU" tendency.

Among IUs constituted of complex sentences, a very salient disparity in frequency can be easily detected between those with complement clauses (49% of all multi-clausal IUs) and those with adverbial clauses (1% of all multi-clausal IUs). In fact, out of the 131 adverbial clauses coded in the database, only 5 are situated within the same IU with the main clause, and 128 constitute independent IUs by themselves. Complement clauses, on the other hand, are very rarely separated from their complement-taking predicates (henceforth CTP's). Only 10 cases have been discovered in the database to have the complement clause and its CTP respectively situated in separate IUs. Such a disparity can be adequately accounted for by the factor of "distance" as proposed by Croft (1995). That is, while a complement clause serves as an argument to the main verb, an adverbial clause has no direct syntactic relation to the main clause and is an adjunct. The proximity principle of iconicity summarized by Givón (1990) can fully characterize the interrelationships:

> "Entities that are closer together functionally, conceptually, or cognitively will be placed closer together at the code level, i.e., temporally or spatially." (Givón 1990: 970)

In other words, whether a subordinate clause and its main clause are packaged within the same IU can be determined by the functional distance between the two clauses.

As already shown in §4.3.2.2.3, Cogtse has IUs made up

of clauses that are juxtaposed without any overt linkage marker that denotes coordination or consecutivization, or any morphosyntactic marking that signals dependency of one clause on the other. However, when text relations between the juxtaposed clauses are scrutinized, strong rhetorical links are observed (based on the relational categories summarized in Matthiessen & Thompson 1988). Of the 40 occurrences of juxtaposed-clause IUs in the narratives, 20 (i.e., 50%) are internally unified by a circumstance relation. For example, in (185), the first clause in the IU, *ndzok to-ndo ˆ-s* 'slightly PFV-there.be₂-PST' lays out a circumstance for the second clause, *mɐj ka-pe ˆt* 'again NMZL:GP-bring'.

(185) Narrative06

96. {ndzok tondos [todzon] } {mɐj} {kapet}

ndzok	to-ndô-s	(Clause 1)
slightly	PFV-there.be$_2$-PST	
mɐj	ka-pêt	(Clause 2)
again	NMZL-bring$_1$	

'(When) there is quite a lot of (herb) (on the pad), we bring it (i.e., the herb) to the sack'

A number of juxtaposed-clause IUs are observed to hold a background relation, as exemplified below by (186).

(186) Narrative08

141. (0.3) a {tə^rgok rokaktor} {wandʐj̨} {{{tʰɐmtʃɐt
kənəwo} tə} ana}

a	tə-rgok	ro-ka-ktor	(Clause 1)
PART	N-grain	PFV-NMZL-sprinkle$_2$	

wa-ndʐĵ		stʰɐmtʃɐt kə-^{12}nəwô=tə=ana	(Clause 2)
3SG:POS-partnerall		NMZL-be.sick$_1$=TOP=DM	

'(The lama) sprinkled grains, his partners were all sick'

Note that the two clauses in this IU are both medial clauses of a clause chain (the final clause is three IUs away, in IU144). In this IU, it is the lama's sprinkling of grains that made the partners sick. The first clause, which describes the sprinkling of grains, thus provides background information (i.e., the cause) for the incident described in the second clause.

There are 6 juxtaposed-clause IUs within which no rhetorical meaning is discerned between the clauses. However, in these IUs, the clauses together provide contextual information for the following mono-clausal IU. For example:

---

[12] It appears that the nominalizer kə- is used here because 'his partners' refers to ghosts, which are not human. In addition, it has been observed that, if the subject of a chained medial clause is a lama or monk, the human plural nominalizer ka- is applied even when the subject is singular (probably to show respect). Cf. §0 for the definition and examples of the clause chain.

(187) Narrative11

20. {ʃi^ste kətʃaɲ ʃo kawapupu tə wuʒi}

ʃistê	kə-tʃã-ɲ=ʃô	ka-wapupu=tə=wuʒi
so.very	NMZL-be.destitute₁-PL=always	NMZL-have.many.children₁=TOP=DM

'(The destitute family) are always so very destitute, have so many children'

21. {kəməzdək^pɐn te nəŋo wuŋkʰu}

kə-məzdəkpên	te	nə-ŋos=wəŋkʰu
NMZL-be.pitiful₁	one	OBV-COP₁=SUB

'(They are) a pitiful (family)'

The juxtaposed (chained medial) clauses in IU20 are not rhetorically related to each other. However, together they serve a common purpose-- to produce background information, so that people know why the destitute family is pitiful.

The multi-clausal IUs examined for this discussion reveal that an IU can have more than one clause if the clauses hold a strong rhetorical, functional, and grammatical link in between. In other words, although such IUs do not go with the "one clause per IU" tendency, the clauses within are usually used to represent parts that compose a unified situation. The constraint of "one new idea per IU", which underlies the "one clause per

IU" tendency (Chafe 1994), is therefore not violated.

4.6. Prosodic Correlations to Discourse and Grammar: Some Observations

As demonstrated in Chapter 3, Cogtse intonation is derived by a set of distinct yet interacting tonal rules. In other words, it is not "overlaid" upon the IU for discourse-grammatical reasons. In the present study, some prosody-discourse and prosody-grammar correspondences are observed respectively in extrapropositional expressions and the quotative construction. Instead of involving any overlaid intonational patterns, which are not available in Cogtse, these correlations either require none of the intonation-related tonal rules, or only one of them (i.e., the prosodic accent).

4.6.1. Extrapropositional Expressions

Extrapropositional IUs tend to be organizational, interactional, and make little ideational contribution to the content of speech (Pierrehumbert & Hirschberg 1990; Wennerstrom 2001). Extrapropositional expressions in Cogtse, like those in English, tend to be produced with low pitch throughout. I analyze such extrapropositional IUs as having no tonal rules applied to them to derive surface contours. They are not marked for any intonational features, and are produced with a default low tone. Consider example (188) below. IU139 carries an extrapropositional meaning. While the preceding and following IUs (i.e., IU138, IU140, IU141) surface with intonational patterns derived by related tonal rules, IU39 is produced with low pitch.

(188) Narrative04

138. {tawat te} {kɐ^lwɐk ptʂe} {wuti mənaŋorə}
     [L-H H L-H L L-H H-H-H-L
     ta-wat te kɐ-lwêk ptʂê wɐti=mənaŋorə
     N-mountainone NMZL:GP-climb.over then there=TOP

'We climbed over a mountain, and there'

139. tʰe mərme
     [L L-L]
     tʰe mərmê
     what be.named

'What's it called'

140. {tsʰaluŋ}
     [L-H]
     tsʰaluŋ
     PLN

'Tshlung'

141. {kə^loɲɲeɲe tə} {ŋa ŋəkanəmʃi} {wuti} {kəɲi kə^do=
wuŋkʰu rə}
[L-H-L-L   L   H   L-H-H-L   L-H   L-H   L-LH   L-L   L
kəlôk=ɲeɲe=tə   ŋa   ŋə-ka-nəmʃi
shepherd=PL=TOP   1SG   1SG:POS-NMZL:PAT-know₁
wəti   kə-ɲî   kə-do=wəŋkʰu=rə
there   NMZL-live₁PL-there.be=3SG:POS-back=TOP

'There lived some shepherds that I knew, so…'

Compare the pitch track of IU139 with that of the other
IUs in Figure 1. 3:

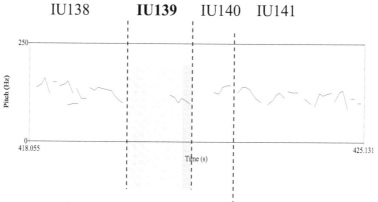

Figure 1. 3 F0 track of Example (188)

4.6.2. Prosody-Grammar Correlation in the Quotative Construction

We now turn to the use of a prosodic element within a defined syntactic construction.

As already shown in §3.2.3, terminal directions of the IU contour are not regularly associated with any particular grammatical construction. The boundary tone H% is not applied to mark aspects of syntactic structure; rather, it seems to denote some discourse-functional meaning.

There is, however, one prosodic pattern that has been observed to be clearly (though not uniquely and obligatorily) associated to the quotative construction. In Cogtse, the quotative construction is formed by a direct quote followed by a quotative verb. The quote does not come with a complementizer. Sometimes it can end with a topicalizer =*tə*, but more often there is no intervening morpheme to mark the boundary between the quote and the quotative verb. The intonational configuration of the quotative construction also involves prosodic phrasing, accent placement and the boundary tone. However, quite frequently, a prosodic accent is placed at the end of the quote. For example (the direct quote is enclosed in square brackets):

(189) Narrative18

59. {no} {kətəs tə^tʃʰe=n tatsəs}
[no   kətə-s   tə-tʃʰê-n]   tâ-tsəs3
2SG   where-ALL   2-go$_1$-2SG   PFV:EVI-say$_1$

'"Where are you going" (the old man) said'

It should be noted that the accent placement is consistently realized on the last syllable of the quote. Consider Example (190) In IU47, the quotative construction is followed by a connective and a demonstrative, but the prosodic accent still falls on the last syllable of the direct quote.

(190) Narrative07

→ 47. {{wutə wuptʃɐkɐ} to^pu= toktsis naŋo ptşerə}
{wujiɐ−}
[wətə   wə-ptʃɐkê   to-pɐ-w]
that   3SG:POS-materials   IMP-do$_1$-TR
to-kə-tsis   na-ŋôs   ptşêrə   wəɲê
PFV-NMZL-say$_2$ IMPFV:PST-COP$_2$ then   those

48. {topɐŋ}
to-pê-ŋ
PFV-do$_2$=1SG

IUs 47-48: "'Prepare the material (i.e., guns and bullets)" he said, then I did'

Example (191) below shows a quotative construction that has a direct quote embedded within another direct quote; and interestingly, the end of each direct quote receives one prosodic accent.

(191) Narrative07

41. {nɐkəŋ^kʰɐ=n nɐk^tsə=s nɐtsə}
   [[nɐ-kə-ŋkʰɐn]   nɐ-kə-tsəs]   nɐ-tsəs
   OBV-PL-be.plenty₁   OBV-PL-say₁   OBV-say₁

'He said they say (deer) are plenty (there)'
(literally: ""'(deer) are plenty (there)' they said" he said')

In the examples that have been presented so far, direct quotes all end with a verb. Example (192) below will show that, when a quote ends with a discourse marker, the same accent-placement pattern still occurs.

(192) Narrative07

104. {{{jikʰərə= (0.1) skə^rmɐ te karo} masanos ^lu=
tokətsi} naŋos}

[jə-kʰərəskərmê	te	ka-ro	ma-sanos	lu]
1PL:POS-divination	one	NMZL-see₁	NEG-be.willing.to₁	DM
to-kə-tsis-j		na-ŋôs		
PFV-NMZL-say₂-1PL		IMPFV:PST-COP₂		

'"Would you please perform a divination for us?" we said'

One might wonder whether the prosodic accent is placed at the end of the direct quote, or whether it actually falls before the quotative verb. Example (193) below clearly shows that it is the end of the quote, not right before the quotative verb, that the prosodic accent is placed.

(193) Narrative18

14. {ʃtə^ksə kɔsatʃa ^tə= ʃo naktsis pre}

[ʃtə-kəsân	kə-sa-tʃâ=tə]=ʃô	na-kə-tsis	prê
this-way	NMZL-1-be.destitute=TOP=always	IMPFV:PST-NMZL-say₂	then

'"(Why) am I so destitute?" (she) kept saying'

In this example, the topicalizer =tə signifies the end of the quote; the adverbial enclitic ʃô 'always, continuously' is used to modify the quotative verb, so is not a part of the quote. Therefore, although the adverbial enclitic immediately precedes the quotative verb, the accent does not fall on it, but on the topicalizer.

There are of course unpredictable cases in which the prosodic pattern demonstrated above does not occur. In example (194), no prosodic accent falls on the last syllable of *nə-po-sə-pɐ-w* 'IMP-come.and-CAUS-do-TR', which is the end of the direct quote.

(194) Narrative14

53. {^wɐjtʃin te nəposəpu nɐktsə} {ptʂer}

[wɐ́jtʃin   te   nə-po-sə-pɐ-w]   nɐ-kə-tsəs   ptʂêrə
gastroscopy one   IMP-come.and-CAUS-do$_1$-TR   OBV-PL-say$_1$ then

'"Come and have a gastroscopy examination" they said, then'

However, in the narratives examined, quotative constructions with this special accent-placement pattern tremendously outnumber quotative constructions without it. Table 4.9 shows the prevalence of quotative constructions that have the special accent-placement pattern.[13]

---

13 In calculating the distribution, the super-complex IUs that end with a matrix quotative verb are also included.

	Quotative Constructions		
	w/ special prosodic accent	w/o special prosodic accent	Total
Tokens	**122**	36	162
Percentage	**78%**	22%	100%

Table 4.9 Quotative construction with and without the special accent placement

It should be noted that not all subordinate clauses are observed to have similar correlations between prosody and syntax. Other kinds of complement clauses, for example, do not show regular accent placement that marks the boundary between the end of the complement clause and the complement-taking predicate. Consider (195) below (with the complement clause enclosed in square brackets). In this complex sentence, the verb in the complement clause *ka-sat* carries an infinitive nominalizer *ka-*.

(195) Narrative03

171. (0.5) {təwam ʒi} {ɹɐspɐ} {te kasat} nɐɾɲow}
    [tə-wam=ʒi   ɹɐspɐ   te   ka-sat]   nɐ-ɾɲo-w
    N-bear=also quite.a.few one NMZL-kill₁ PFV-experience;taste₂-TR

'(He) has also killed quite a few bears (literally: He experienced killing quite a few bears).'

The distribution of complement clauses with and without a

prosodic accent on the final syllable is given below in Table 4.10:

	Other Complement Clauses		
	w/ accent on the last syll	w/o accent on the last syll	Total
Number of IUs	38	99	137
Percentage	28%	72%	100%

Table 4.10 Complement clauses with a prosodic accent
on the last syllable

All these facts seem to suggest that the quotative construction has developed a regular prosodic pattern, which distinguishes it from other complementation constructions.[14]

4.7. Summary and Conclusion

This chapter started with proposing a transcription convention to transcribe Cogtse natural discourse. Then, the grammatical taxonomy of the Cogtse IU was examined. IUs were grammatically categorized based on six coding criteria. Five major subtypes of non-clausal IUs (i.e., nominal, discourse markers, adverbials, ideophones, onomatopoetic), five major subtypes of mono-clausal IUs (i.e., fully-finite clauses, nominalized finite clauses, non-finite clauses, adverbial clauses, and relative clauses), as well as four major subtypes of

---

14 Mithun (2009) reports a Mohawk case in which prosody is used to signify subordination. Readers are referred to Mithun 2009 for more details about related phenomena in Mohawk.

multi-clausal IUs (i.e., complex sentences, super-complex sentences, juxtaposed clauses, and sequential sentences) were observed in the 3,030 IUs examined.

While surrounding contexts were considered for the functional interpretation of the nominalized finite clause, its special function in clause-chaining was discovered. The Cogtse clause chain is crucially distinct from converb construction in that all its medial clauses are finite.

The distribution of the structural types suggests that the preferred syntactic structure of the Cogtse IU is the clause. A high proportion of clausal IUs does not go with the "one clause per IU" tendency as discovered by Chafe (1980). Nonetheless, it is shown that, if the clauses within a multi-clausal IU hold a strong link in rhetorical relations and/or show tight syntactic integration, the clauses very possibly represent parts of a unified situation. The more fundamental constraint of "one new idea per IU" (Chafe 1994) is thus not violated.

This study also reveals two prosodic correlations to discourse and grammar. Extrapropositional expressions in Cogtse, like those in English, tend to be produced with low pitch throughout. In addition, an interesting prosody-grammar correspondence was observed in Cogtse quotative constructions. It was observed that the quotative complement is regularly (though not always) produced with a prosodic accent on the last syllable. This special association between accent placement and the quotative construction does not occur as regularly in other types of complementation constructions. It is assumed that this prosodic pattern has developed to distinguish the quotative construction from other complementation constructions.

Chapter 5
Conclusion

5.0. Introduction

The present study has explored the phonological properties and grammatical taxonomy of the Intonation Unit, the basic prosodic unit, in Cogtse spontaneous narratives. It started with a phonological analysis of Cogtse word prosody, then segmented the narratives collected into IUs using six prosodic features. The reliability of the prosodic cues was confirmed by inter-rater reliability tests. The most crucial prosodic feature, intonation, was analyzed using notions and methods adopted from the autosegmental/metrical (AM) theory. Finally, grammatical exponents were analyzed and coded for all the IUs that were segmented prosodically.

The narratives used in this study were collected in spontaneous interview sessions. All of the participants were native speakers of Cogtse Rgyalrong from the same village in Cogtse Township. They contributed twenty stories of folklore as well as those concerning their own lives and past experiences. The narratives were transcribed by the author in the field with the help of Dongfang Yang, the main consultant. In addition to the spontaneous data, the present project also examined constructed examples (elicited single words as well as syntactic constructions) to explore the word-prosody system, as well as the relationship between tone and intonation.

Previous analyses of Cogtse word prosody were reviewed. In particular, the approaches involving tone and pitch-accent were inspected against a typological context, and then compared with the privative tonal system that is proposed for Cogtse word prosody in the present study.

For prosodic segmentation, six prosodic cues were chosen to segment the narratives into IUs. The cues were identified auditorily. Inter-rater reliability tests were undertaken using excerpts extracted from the narratives. The results showed that in segmentation the two participants in the tests were able to achieve a better than chance agreement rate by cuing in the prosodic cues.

Meanwhile, an intonational analysis was also undertaken on the same set of data. Based on the autosegmental/metrical (AM) theory, it was figured out that three phonological tones could appropriately describe the contour shape over each IU.

After all these results were gained, all the Cogtse narratives were segmented into IUs by the author. Each IU was marked for pitch contour using the transcription convention proposed in §3.3.2.

The IUs were then coded for structural type based on six criteria (cf. §4.1). Each structural type identified in the data was briefly described (§4.2). The distribution of the structural types and related discussion were provided (§4.3). Meanwhile, this study also investigated possible prosody-grammar relationships, and an interesting correspondence was discovered.

The remainder of this chapter will be organized as follows. The main findings of the present study will be summarized in §§5.1-5.6, in addressing the research questions posed for Cogtse in the introduction (§1.5). Then, in the final section (§5.7), I will recapitulate the primary contributions of this study, identify its limitations, and present some suggestions for future research.

5.1. RQ1: How can Cogtse word prosody be best characterized? Is it tonal, pitch-accented, or both?

Cogtse word prosody can be characterized in strictly tonal terms. It exhibits a tonal contrast between /Ø/ and /HL/. In the lexicon, only /HL/ has to be specified, then phonological rules can derive the surface melody of lexically falling-toned and toneless words. Toneless words must be realized with either Surface-Melody 1 or Surface-Melody 2, which are sensitive to distinct grammatical contexts.

Although a "tone and pitch-accent" approach works well for Cogtse, they weaken phonological theory in terms of typology and analytical methodology. Section 2.3 presents details about the strictly tonal analysis, with all the grammatical contexts that involve tonal variations presented in §2.3.3.

5.2. RQ2: How does prosody organize speech into basic units?

Cogtse speech can be organized into IUs using six prosodic cues i.e., pause, final lengthening, anacrusis, pitch reset, coherent intonational contour, and final creaky voice. Among the cues, coherent intonation contours are observed over the entire IU, while the other cues are situated on the boundary.

The twenty narratives of ninety-one minutes and five seconds in total were segmented into 3, 253 IUs. Sections 3.1-3.3 provide the relevant details, including the definition of the cues, inter-rater reliability tests for segmentation consistency, and the results of prosodic segmentation.

5.3. RQ3: What are the contour shapes observed on the Cogtse IU? How are they best described?

This study demonstrates that the surface IU contours result from the operation and placement of three phonological parameters. This proposed phonological model allows us to derive the pitch shape of an IU based on the parsing of prosodic phrases, the placement of the prosodic accent, and the presence or absence of the boundary tone H%.

Therefore, unlike the contour patterns observed in many languages, Cogtse contour shapes cannot be categorized by their terminal directions. This is because the terminal tones result from the interactions among the three phonological tones, rather than being "overlaid" upon an IU for discoursefunctional reasons. The intonational analysis of intonation is presented in §3.2.

5.4. RQ4: What is the relationship between tone and intonation?

When discussing the relationship between tone and intonation, people usually talk about whether lexical tone is maintained or overridden by intonation. The analysis of Cogtse intonation shows that lexical tone can be maintained in an intonational contour if it is not overridden by surface tones that are derived by phrasal rules, accent placement, or the boundary tone H%. How words are grouped into prosodic phrases is not determined by grammatical structures in most cases (except the accent placement in the quotative construction, see §4.6.2 and §5.6 below). Rather, they seem to vary for different discourse functions, which remain to be fully explored in future research. Cf. §3.2 for related discussions in the intonational analysis.

5.5. RQ5: What are the grammatical exponents of Cogtse IUs? What does the distribution of the structural types tell us about the grammatical organization of Cogtse natural speech?

Five major subtypes of non-clausal IUs (i.e., nominal,

discourse markers, adverbials, ideophones, onomatopoetic), five major subtypes of mono-clausal IUs (i.e., fully-finite clauses, nominalized finite clauses, non-finite clauses, adverbial clauses, and relative clauses), as well as four major subtypes of multi-clausal IUs (i.e., complex sentences, super-complex sentences, juxtaposed clauses, and sequential sentences) were identified in the database. The distribution of these structural types shows that the preferred syntactic structure of Cogtse IUs is the clause. A surprisingly high proportion of multi-clausal IUs (31%) do not follow the "one clause per IU" tendency observed by Chafe (1980) in English. Nonetheless, it has been shown that, if the clauses within a multi-clausal IU show a strong link in rhetorical relations and/or tight integration, the "one clause per IU" constraint can be violated.

5.6. RQ6: Is there any salient correlation between prosody and grammatical or discourse functions?

In terms of prosody-disourse correspondence, it was discovered that extrapropositional expressions in Cogtse tend to be produced with low pitch throughout. I analyze such extrapropositional IUs as having no tonal rules applied to them to derive surface contours. Cf. §4.6.1 for more details.

Meanwhile, a rather regular grammarprosody correspondence is observed in the quotative construction. That is, a prosodic accent is very frequently (though not uniquely and obligatorily) placed on the last syllable of a direct quote that immediately precedes the quotative verb in the quotative construction. This seems to suggest that the quotative construction has developed a regular prosodic pattern, which distinguishes it from other complementation constructions. Cf. §4.6.1 for the discussion of this prosodygrammar correspondence.

5.7. Contribution, Limitation, and Future Research

The present study has demonstrated how speech can be organized into basic prosodic units (IUs), and what grammatical structures can be contained in the IU in Cogtse. It is the first extensive research on prosody and grammar based on real-time speech in Rgyalrong, as well as the first study of tone and intonation in a language that has a privative tonal system of zero versus Falling tone.

However, this research is limited in the sense that the study focuses only on prosody and grammar in single IUs. The restriction was adopted to avoid unnecessary complications while the most basic prosodic and grammatical patterns were teased out. Now that a clearer picture of these patterns exists, one can venture beyond the individual IUs.

One important question that definitely deserves future research is how transitional continuity is presented in Cogtse.

Transitional continuity is concerned with the prosodic cues that indicate whether the speaker will continue or finish his/her speech. Future studies on this topic need to address two issues. One is the identification and definition of "speaker's intention for further speech". For this, conversational data will be required to provide interactional information that infer the speaker's intention if it is not specified explicitly in the speech. On the other hand, as mentioned in §3.4, the intonational variations, especially the different terminal pitch directions observed in Cogtse, are not associated with the transitional-continuity classes of final, continuing and appeal. Du Bois et al. (1993) note that the marking of finality can be language-specific and does not have to be restricted to terminal pitch directions; therefore, a future study on Cogtse prosody will have to determine the prosodic features that correlate with the transitional-continuity classes. At this stage, a pilot study I have undertaken shows that, like IUs in Mandarin (Tao 1996: 47-49), Cogtse IUs can also be further grouped into declination units. IUs within one declination unit are all situated under one common declination line, and the last IU in the declination unit can be identified as a final IU. It should be noted, however, that declination and the declination unit are acoustically defined ('t Hart et al. 1990; Ladd 1984; 1986; 1988; 1993; Pierrehumbert 1980; Schuetze-Coburn et al. 1991), so the analysis of declination units will involve acoustic studies of related prosodic cues and instrumental measurement.

In addition to the above-mentioned possible extensions from the present research, another worthwhile direction for future research concerns discourse structure and discourse content, in particular the prosodic cues that signify discourse structuring, as well as prosodic patterns that vary with differences in discourse meaning. The present research is able to describe intonational patterns in phonological terms, but it did not determine what triggers the variations. One thing that is known is that grammar is not a primary determinant, and discourse functions and interactional meanings could be possible candidates. Systematically investigating these factors and their relationships to prosody will surely produce crucial insights.

REFERENCES

't Hart, Johan, René Collier & Antonie Cohen. 1990. *A Perceptual Study of Intonation*. Cambridge: Cambridge University Press.

Aikhenvald, Alexandra Y. & R.M.W Dixon (eds) 2006. *Serial Verb Constructions: A Cross-Linguistic Typology*. Oxford and New York: Oxford University Press.

Beckman, Mary E. & G. M. Ayers. 1994. "Guidelines for ToBI labelling". In *Online MS and accompanying files available at http://www.ling.ohio-state.edu/~tobi/ame_tobi*.

Beckman, Mary E., Julia Hirschberg & Stefanie Shattuck-Hufnagel. 2005. "The original ToBI system and the evolution of the ToBI framework". *The Phonology of Intonation and Phrasing*, ed. by S.-A. Jun, 9-54. New York: Oxford University Press.

Beckman, Mary E. & Janet B. Pierrehumbert. 1986. "Intonation structure in Japanese and English". *Phonology Yearbook* 3.255-309.

Beckman, Mary & Julia Hirschberg. 1994. *The ToBI annotation conventions*. Ohio State University.

Bickel, Balthasar. 1998. "Review article: Converbs in cross-linguistic perspective". *Linguistic Typology* 2.381-97.

Bisang, Walter. 1995. "Verb serialization and converbs: differences and similarities". *Converbs in Crosslinguistic Pers-*

pective, ed. by M. Haspelmath, and Ekkehard Konig, 137-88. Berlin: Mouton de Gruyter.

Bolinger, Dwight L. 1989. *Intonation and Its Uses: Melody in Grammar and Discourse*. London: Edward Arnold.

Chafe, Wallace L. 1980. "The deployment of consciousness in the production of a narrative". *The Pear Stories: Cognitive, Cultural and Linguistic Aspects of Narrative Poduction*, ed. by W.L. Chafe, 9-50. Norwood: Ablex Publishing.

—. 1987. "Cognitive constraints on information flow". *Coherence and Grounding in Discourse, ed.* by R. Tomlin, 21-52. Amsterdam and Philadephia: John Benjamins.

—. 1988. "Prosodic and functional units of language". *Talking Data: Tanscription and Coding in Discourse Reseach*, ed. by J.A. Edwards, and Martin D. Lampert, 33-44. Hillside, NJ: Lawrence Erlbaum Associates.

—. 1993. "Linking intonation units in spoken English". *Clause Combining in Grammar and Discourse*, ed. by J.H.a.S. A.Thompson, 1-28. Amsterdam and Philadelphia: John Benjamins.

—. 1994. *Discourse, Consciousness, and Time: The Flow and Displacement of Conscious experience in speaking and writing*. Chicago: University of Chicago Press.

—. 1996. "How consciousness shapes language." *Pragmatics and Cognition* 4.35-54.

—. 1997. "The interplay of syntax and prosody in the expression of thoughts". *Proceedings of the 23rd Annual Meeting of the Berkeley Linguistic Society*, ed. by M.L.J.a.J.L. Moxley, 389-401. Berkeley: Berkeley Linguistic Society.

—. 1998. "Language and the flow of thought". *The New Psychology of Language: Cognitive and Functional Approaches to Languge Structure*, ed. by M. Tomasello. Mahwah, NJ: Lawrence Erlbaum.

Clements, George N & Samuel Jay Keyser. 1983. *CV Phonology*. Cambridge: MIT Press.

Croft, William. 1995. *Intonation units and grammatical structure*. Linguistics 33.839-82.

Cruttenden, Alan. 1997. *Intonation*. Cambridge (UK): Cambridge Univesity Press.

Crystal, David. 1969. *Prosodic System and Intonation in English*. Cambridge: Cambridge University Press.

Cumming, Susanna & Tsuyoshi Ono. 1997. "Discourse and grammar". *Discourse as Structure and Process*, ed. by T.A. Dijk, 112-37. London: Sage.

Donohue, Mark. 1997. "Tone systems in New Guinea". *Linguistic Typology* 1.347-86.

Du Bois, John W. 1987. "The discourse basis of ergativity". *Language* 63.805-55.

Du Bois, John W., Susanna Cumming, Stephan Schuetze-Coburn & Danae Paolino. 1992. *Discourse Transcription*.: University of California, Santa Barbara, Department of Linguistics.

—. 1993. "Outline of discourse transcription." *Talking Data: Trancription and Coding in Discourse Research*, ed. by J.A.E.a.M.D. Lampert, 45-90. Hillside, NJ: Lawrence Erlbaum Associates.

Dung, Đỗ The, Tran Thien Huong and Georges Boulakia. 1998. Intonation in Vietnamese. *Intonation Systems: A Survey of Twenty Languages*, ed. by D.H.a.A.D. Cristo, 395-416. Cambridge (UK): Cambridge University Press.

Foley, William A. & Mike Olson. 1985. "Clausehood and verb serialization." *Grammar Inside and Outside the Clause: Some Approaches to Theory from the Field*, ed. by J. Nichols & A. Woodbury, 17-60. New York: Cambridge University Press.

Foley, William A. & Robert Van Valin. 1984. *Functional Syntax and Universal Grammar*. Cambridge: Cambridge University Press.

Ford, Cecilia & Sandra A. Thompson. 1996. "Interactional units in conversation: Syntactic, intonational, and pragmatic resources for the management of turns." *Interaction and Grammar*, ed. by E. Ochs, E.A. Schegloff & S.A. Thompson, 134-84. Cambridge: Cambridge University Press.

Garding, Eva & Jan-Olof Svantesson. 1994. "An introductory study of tone and intonation in a Lao dialect." *Acta Linguistica Hafniensia* 27.219-33.

Gates, Jesse. 2014. Situ in Situ: *Towards a Dialectology of Jiarong (rGyalrong): LINCOM GmbH.*

Genetti, Carol. 2007a. *A Grammar of Dolakha Newar* Berlin: Mouton de Gruyter.

—.2007b. *Syntax and prosody: interacting coding systems in Dolakha Newar*. SEALS XIII: Papers from the 13th meeting of the Southeast Asian Linguistics Society (2003), ed. by K. Adams & P. Sidwell. Canberra: Pacific Linguistics.

Genetti, Carol, Alec R. Coupe, Ellen Bartee, Kristine Hildebrandt & You-Jing Lin. 2008. "Syntactic aspects of nominalization in five Tibeto-Burman languages of the Himalayan area." *Linguistics of the Tibeto-Burman Area* 31.97-143.

Genetti, Carol & Keith Slater. 2004. "An analysis of syntax and prosody interactions in a Dolakha Newar Rendition of the Mahabharata." *Himalayan Linguistics* 1.1-91.

Genetti, Carol. 2005. 2005. "The participial construction of Dolakhā Newar: syntactic implications of an Asian converb." *Studies in Language* 29.35-87.

Givón, Talmy. 1990. *Syntax: A Functional-Typological Introduction*. Amsterdam and Philadelphia: John Benjamins.

Goldsmith, John. 1976. *Autosegmental Phonology:* MIT PhD Dissertation.

Gong, Xun. 2014. "The personal agreement system of Zbu Rgyalrong (Ngyalrsu Variety)." *Transactions of Philological Society* 112.17.

Gordon, Matthew. 2005. "Intonation phonology of Chickasaw." *Prosodic Typology: The Phonology of Intonation and Phras-*

ing, ed. by S.-A. Jun, 301-30. New York: Oxford University Press.

Gussenhoven, Carlos. 2004. *The Phonology of Tone and Intonation.* Cambridge (UK): Cambridge University Press.

Halliday, M. A. K. 1967. *Intonation and Grammar in British English.* The Hague: Mouton.

—.1985. *An Introduction to Functional Grammar.* London: Edward Arnold.

Haspelmath, Marin. 1995. "The converb as a cross-linguistically valid category." *Converbs in Cross-Linguistic Perspective: Structure and Meaning of Adverbial Verb Forms,* ed. by M. Haspelmath & E. König, 1-56. Berlin and New York: Mouton de Gruyter.

Hayes, Bruce. 1989. *Compensatory lengthening in moraic phonology.* Linguistic Inquiry 20.253-306.

Hirst, Daniel & Albert Di Cristo. 1998. *Intonation Systems: A Survey of Twenty Languages.* New York: Cambridge University Press.

Holton, Gary. 2005. *Pitch, tone, and intonation in Tanacross.* Athabaskan Prosody, ed. by S. Hargus & K. Rice, 249-75. Amsterdam: John Benjamins.

Hopper, Paul J. 1995. "The category 'event' in natural discourse and logic." *Discourse Grammar and Typology: Papers in Honor of John W.M. Verhaar,* ed. by W. Abraham, T. Givón & S.A. Thompson, 139-50. Amsterdam and Philadelphia: John Benjamins.

Hsieh, Feng-fan. 1999. *Theoretical Aspects of Zhuokeji r Gyalrong Phonology.* Hsinchu: National Tsing Hua University MA Thesis.

Hu, Chenying. 2016. *Xiaojin Jiarongyu zhong de mingwuhua (Nominalization in Xiaojin Rgyalrong):* Peking University.

Huang, Liangrong & Hongkai Sun (eds) 2002. *Han Jiarong Cidian (A Chinese-rGyalrong Dictionary).* Beijing: Minzu Chubanshe (Ethnic Publishing House).

Hyman, Larry M. 1985. *A Theory of Phonological Weight.* Dordrecht: Foris.

—. 2006. *Word prosodic typology.* Phonology 23.225-57.

—. 2007. "How (not) to do phonological typology: the case of pitch-accent." *UC Berkeley Phonology Lab Annual Reporting.*654-85.

Iwasaki, Shoichi & Hongyin Tao. 1993. "A comparative study of the structure of the intonation unit in English, Japanese, and Mandarin Chinese." Paper presented to the the Annual Meeting of the Linguistics Society of America, Los Angeles, CA, 1993.

Jacques, Guillaume. 2008. *Jiarongyu Yanjiu (A Study of Rgyalrong).* Beijing: The Ethnic Publishing House.

—. 2010a. "The inverse in Japhug Rgyalrong." *Language and Linguistics* 11.127-57.

—. 2010b. "The origin of the reflexive prefix in Rgyalrong languages." *Bulletin of the School of Oriental and African Studies* 73.261-68.

—. 2012a. "Agreement morphology: th case of Ryalrongic and Kiranti." *Language and Linguistics* 13.83-116.

—. 2012b. *Argument demotion in Japhug Rgyalrong*. Ergativity, Valency and Voice, ed. by G. Authier & K. Haude, 199-225. Berlin: Mouton de Gruyter.

—. 2012c. *From denominal derivation to incorporation*. Lingua 122.1207-31.

—. 2013a. "Applicative and tropative derivations in Japhug Rgyalrong." *Linguistics of the Tibeto-Burman Area* 36.1-13.

—. 2013b. "Ideophones in Japhug Rgyalrong." *Anthropological Linguistics* 55.256-87.

—. 2014a. "Clause linking in Japhug Rgyalrong." *Linguistics of the Tibeto-Burman Area* 37.263-327.

—. 2014b. "Denominal affixes as sources of antipassive markers in Japhug Rygalrong." *Lingua* 138.1-22.

—. 2015a. "The origin of the causatie prefix in Rgyalrong languages and its implication for Proto-Sino-Tibetan reconstruction." *Folia Linguistica Historiica* 36.165-98.

—. 2015b. "The spontaneous-autobenfactive prefix in Japhug Rgyalrong." *Linguistics of the Tibeto-Burman Area* 38. 279-91.

—. 2016. "Subjects, objects and relativization in Japhug." *Journal of Chinese Linguistics* 44.1-28.

—. 2018. *Dictionnaire Japhug-chinois-français*.

Jacques, Guillaume, Yunfan Lai, Anton Antonov & Lobsang

Nima. 2017. Stau. The *Sino-Tibetan Languages*, 2nd Ed., ed. by G. Thurgood & R. LaPolla, 597-614. New York: Taylor & Francis.

Jun, Sun-Ah. 2005a. "Korean intonational phonology." *Prosodic Typology: The Phonology of Intonation and Phrasing*, ed. by S.-A. Jun, 201-29. New York: Oxford University Press.

—.(ed.) 2005b. *Prosodic Typology: The Phonology of Intonation and Phrasing*. New York: Oxford University Press.

Kilian-Hatz, Christa 2001. "Universality and diversity: ideophones from Baka and Kxoe." *Ideophones*, ed. by E.F.K. Voeltz & C. Kilian-Hatz, 155-63. Amsterdam: John Benjamins.

Kin, Peng et al. 1957-58. *Jiarongyu Suomohuade yuyin he xingtai (Phonology and morphology in Suomo Rgyalrong)*. Yuyan Yanjiu 2.

Kratochvil, Paul. 1998. "Intonation in Beijing Chinese." *Intonation Systems: A Survey of Twenty Languages*, ed. by D. Hirst & A.D. Cristo, 417-31. Cambridge (UK): Cambridge University Press.

Ladd, D. Robert. 1984. "Declination: a review and some hypotheses." *Phonology Yearbook* 1.311-40.

—.1986. "Intonational phrase: the case for recursive prosodic structure." *Phonology Yearbook* 3.311-40.

—.1988. "Declination "reset" and the hierarchical organization of utterances." *Journal of Acoustical Society of America* 84.530-44.

—. 1993. "On the theoretical status of "the baseline" in modeling intonation." *Language and Speech* 36.435-51.

—. 1996. *Intonational Phonology*. Cambridge: Cambridge University Press.

Lai, Yunfan. 2013. *Erehuade fuyin chongdie (Consonant reduplication in Ere)*. Minzu Yuwen 6.12-18.

—. 2015. "The person agreement system of Wobzi Lavrung (Rgyalrongic, Tibeto-Burman)." *Transactions of Philological Society* 113.271-85.

—. 2016. "Causativization in Wobzi and other Khroskyabs dialects." *Cahiers de Linguistique-Asie Orientale* 45.28.

—. 2017. *Grammaire du Khroskyabs de Wobzi:* Sorbonne Paris Cité.

Langacker, Ronald W. 2003. "Constructional integration, grammaticization, and serial verb constructions." *Language and Linguistics* 4.251-78.

Li, Yafei. 1991. "On deriving serial verb constructions." *Serial verbs: Grammatical, Comparative and Cognitive Approaches*, ed. by C. Lefebvre, 103-35. Amsterdam: John Benjamins.

Liberman, Mark & Janet Pierrehumbert. 1984. "Intonational invariance under changes in pitch range and length." *Language Sound Structure*, ed. by M. Aronoff & R. Oebrle, 157-233. Cambridge, MA: MIT Press.

Lin, Xiangrong. 1983. "A study of word-formation processes in rGyalrong." *Minzu Yuwen* 3.47-58.

—. 1993. *Jiarongyu yanjiu (A Study of Rgyalrong)* Chengdu: Sichuan Nationality Press.

Lin, You-Jing. 2000. *Tense, Aspect, and Modality Inflection in the Zhuokeji rGyalrong Verb.* Hsinchu: National Tsing Hua University MA Thesis.

—. 2002. "A dimension missed: east and west in Situ rGyalrong orientation marking." *Language and Linguistics* 3.27-42.

—. 2003. "Tense and aspect morphology in the Zhuokeji rGyalrong verb." *Cahiers de Linguistique-Asie Orientale* 32. 245-86.

—. 2009a. "Perfective and imperfective from the same source: directional 'down' in rGyalrong." *Diachronia* 28.28.

—. 2009b. *Units in Zhuokeji rGyalrong Discourse: Prosody and Grammar:* University of California, Santa Barbara PhD Dissertation.

—. 2012. "By no means marginal: Privative tone in Zhuokeji Rgyalrong." *Language and Linguistics* 13.621-62.

—. 2016a. "Xiaojin Jiarongyude Quexing Shengdiaoxitong (The privative word-tone system of Btsanlha Rgyalrong) (in Chinese)." *Essays in Linguistics Yuyanxue Luncong* 54.

—. 2016b. *Zhuokeji Jiarongyu yufabiaozhu wenben (Cogtse Rgyalrong Texts: Fully Analyzed Spontaeous Narratives with an Updated Sketch Grammar of the Language) (in Chinese).* Beijing: Social Sciences Academic Press.

—. 2017a. "How grammar encodes space in Cogtse Rgyalrong." *Himalayan Linguistics* 16.

——. 2017b. "Zhuokeji Jiarongyude Feishiran Jiegou (The Irrealis construction in Cogtse Rgyalrong) (in Chinese)." *Essays in Linguistics Yuyanxue Luncong* 55.

Lin, You-Jing & Erwu Luo. 2003. "Chabao Jiarongyu Dazanghua de quxiangqianzhui yu dongcicigan de bianhua (Orientation prefixes and stem alternation in the Dazang varieity of Japhug rGyalrong)." *Minzu Yuwen* 4.19-29.

Lin, You-Jing, Jackson T.-S Sun & Alvin C. -H Chen. 2012. "Puxi Huo'eryu ruan'ehuade yuyinduili (Contrastive velariz-ation in Puxi Horpa) (in Chinese)." *Essays in Linguistics Yuyanxue Luncong* 45.9.

Longacre, Robert E. 1985. *Sentences as combinations of clauses. Language Typology and Syntactic Description*, ed. by T. Shopen, 235-86. Cambridge: Cambridge University Press.

Lord, Carol. 1993. *Historical Change in Serial Verb Constr-uctions*. Amsterdam: John Benjamins.

Luksaneeyanawin, Sudaporn. 1998. "Intonation in Thai." *Inton-ation Systems: A Survey of Twenty Languages*, ed. by D. Hirst & A.D. Cristo, 376-94. Cambridge (UK): Cambridge University Press.

Matisoff, James A. 1994. "Tone, intonation, and sound symbolism in Lahu: loading the syllable canon." *Sound Symbolism*, ed. by L. Hinton, J. Nichols & J.J. Ohala, 115-28. Cambridge (UK): Cambridge University Press.

Matsumoto, Kazuko. 2003. *Intonation Units in Japanese Conversation.* Amsterdam and Philadelphia: John Benjamins.

Matthiessen, Christian & Sandra A Thompson. 1988. "The structure of discourse and 'subordination'." *Clause Combining in Grammar and Discourse*, ed. by J. Haiman & S.A. Thompson, 275-329. Amsterdam: John Benjamins.

McCarthy, John J. 1979. *Formal Problems in Semitic Phonology and Morphology:* MIT PhD Dissertation.

—. 1981. "A prosodic theory of non-concatenative morphology." *Linguistic Inquiry* 12.373-418.

Mithun, Marianne. 2009. "Re(e)volving complexity: adding intonation." *Syntactic Complexity*, ed. by T. Givón & M. Shibatani, 53-80. Amsterdam.

Nagano, Yasuhiko. 1984. *A Historical Study of the rGyalrong Verb System.* Tokyo: Seishido.

—. 2001. "Cogtse Gyarong." *The Sino-Tibetan Languages*, ed. by G. Thurgood & R. LaPolla, 469-89. London and New York: Routledge.

—. 2003. "Cogtse Gyarong." *The Sino-Tibetan Languages*, ed. by G. Thurgood & R. LaPolla, 469-89. London and New York: Routledge.

Nespor, Mariana & Irene Vogel. 1986. *Prosodic Phonology.* Dordrecht: Foris.

Ngag-dbang-Tshul-khrims, Marielle Prins & Yasuhiko Nagano. 2009. "A lexicon of the rGyalrong bTsanlha dialect:

rGyalrong-Chinese-Tibetan-English." In *A lexicon of the rGyalrong bTsanlha dialect: rGyalrong-Chinese-Tibetan-English*. Osaka: National Museum of Ethnology.

Odden, David. 1999. "Typological issues in tone and stress in Bantu." *Proceedings of the Symposium Cross-Linguistic Studies of Tonal Phenomena: Tonogenesis, Typology, and Related Topics*, Dec. 10-12, 1998, Takinogawa City Hall, Tokyo, ed. by S. Kaji, 187-215. Tokyo: Tokyo University of Foreign Studies.

Park, Joseph Sung-Yul. 2001. "The intonation unit as an interactional resource: an analysis based on prosody-syntax mismatches." *Crossroads of Language, Interaction, and Culture*, ed. by E. Goldknopf, A. Isaac & C. Fuller, 25-38.

—. 2002. "Cognitive and interactional motivations for the intonation unit." *Studies in Language* 26.637-80.

Payne, Thomas. 1991. "Medial clauses and interpropositional relations in Panare." *Cognitive Linguistics* 2.247-82.

Pierrehumbert, Janet B. 1980. *The Phonology and Phonetics of English Intonation:* MIT PhD Dissertation.

Pierrehumbert, Janet B. & Mary E. Beckman. 1988. *Japanese Tone Structure*. Cambridge, MA: MIT Press.

Pierrehumbert, Janet B. & Julia Hirschberg. 1990. "The meaning of intonational contours in discourse." *Intentions in Communication*, ed. by P.R. Cohen, J. Morgan & M.E. Pollack. Cambridge, MA: The MIT Press.

Pitrelli, John F., Mary Beckman & Julia Hirschberg. 1994. "Evaluation of prosodic transcription labeling reliability in the ToBI framework." *Proceedings of the 1992 International Conference on Spoken Language Processing*, 123-26.

Prins, Marielle. 2016. *A grammar of Rgyalrong , Jiǎomùzú (kyom-kyo) Dialects: A Web of Relations*. Leiden: Brill.

Pulleyblank, Douglas. 1986. *Tone in Lexical Phonology*. Dordrecht: D. Reidel.

Qu, Aitang. 1983. *Jiarongyu dongci de rencheng fanchou (The category of person in the rGyalrong verb)*. Minzu Yuwen 4.35-48; 60.

—. 1984. *Jiarongyu gaikuang (Introduction to rGyalrong)*. Minzu Yuwen 2.208-69.

—. 1990. *Jiarongyu de fangyan: fangyan huafen he yuyanshibie (rGyalrong dialects: issues in dialect subclassification and language recognition)*. Minzu Yuwen 4: 1-8; 5: 37-44.

Quirk, Randolph, J. Svartvik, Anne P. Duckworth, J.P.L. Rusiecki & A.J.T. Colin. 1964. "Studies in the correspondence of prosodic to grammatical features in English." *Proceedings of the Ninth International Congress of Linguists, Cambridge, Mass., 1962*, 679-91. The Hague: Mouton.

Schadeberg, Thilo C. 1973. "Kinga: a restricted tone system." *Studies in African Linguistics* 4.23-48.

Schuetze-Coburn, Stephan, Marian Shapley & Elizabeth G.

Weber. 1991. "Units of intonation in discourse: a comparison of acoustic and auditory analyses." *Language and Speech* 34.207-34.

Selkirk, Elizabeth O. 1984. *Phonology and Syntax*. Cambridge: MIT Press.

Shaw, Patricia A. 1985. "Coexisting and competing stress rules in Stoney (Dakota)." *International Journal of American Linguistics* 51.1-18.

Shibatani, Mosayoshi. 1990. *The Languages of Japan*. Cambridge (UK): Cambridge University Press.

Silverman, Kim, Mary Beckman, John Pitrelli, Mori Ostendorf, Colin Wightman, Patti Price, Janet B. Pierrehumbert & Julia Hirschberg. 1992. "ToBI: a standard for labeling English prosody." *Proceedings of the 1992 International Conference on Spoken Language Processing*, 867-70.

Steriade, Donca. 1982. *Greek Prosodies and the Nature of Syllabification:* MIT PhD Dissertation.

Sun, Hongkai, Zengyi Hu & Xing Huang (eds) 2007. *The Languages of China*. Beijing: The Commercial Press.

Sun, Jackson T.-S. 1996. "Caodeng rGyalrong phonology: A first look." *Linguistics of the Tibeto-Burman Area* 17.29-47.

—. 1998. "Nominal morphology in Caodeng rGyalrong." *Bulletin of the Institute of History and Philology* 69. 175-220.

—. 2000a. "Stem alternation in Puxi verb inflection: Toward validating the rGyalrongic Subgroup in Qiangic." *Language and Linguistics* 1.211-32.

—.2003. Caodeng rGyalrong. *The Sino-Tibetan Languages*, ed. by G. Thurgood & R. LaPolla, 490-502. London and New York: Routledge.

—.2007a. The irrealis category in rGyalrong. *Language and Linguistics* 8.797-819.

—.2012. Complementation in Caodeng Rgyalrong. *Language and Linguistics* 13.471-98.

—.2014. "Typology of generic-person marking in Tshobdun Rgyalrong." *Festschrift to Honor South Coblin: Studies in Chinese and Sino-Tibetan Linguistics: Dialect, Phonology, Transcription and Text*, ed. by R. VanNess Simmons & N.A. Van Auken, 225-48. Taipei: Institute of Linguistics, Academia Sinica.

—.2015. Heishuixian Shashiduo Jiarongyu dongci rencheng-fanchoude tedian (Remarkable Features in the Verb Agreement System of Sastod Rgyalrong in Khrochu County) (in Chinese). *Language and Linguistics* 16.19.

—.2017. Tshobdun rGyalrong. *The Sino-Tibetan Languages*, 2nd Ed., ed. by G. Thurgood & R. LaPolla, 557-71. New York: Taylor & Francis.

—.to appear. Evidentials and person. *The Oxford Handbook of Evidentiality*, ed. by A.Y. Aikenvald. Oxford: Oxford Univesity Press.

Sun, Jackson T.-S, Qianzi Tian & Chen-Hao Chiu. 2017. "Shanggu Huo'eryude fashengtai duili (Contrastive phonation in Upper Donggu Horpa) (in Chinese)." *Journal of Chinese Linguistics* 45.19.

Sun, Jackson T.-S. 2000b. "Parallelisms in the verb morphology of Sidaba rGyalrong and Lavrung in rGyalrongic." *Language and Linguistics* 1.161-90.

—.2004. Verb-stem variations in Showu rGyalrong. *Studies on Sino-Tibetan Languages: Papers in Honor of Professor Hwang-Cherng Gong on His Seventieth Birthday*, ed. by Y.-c. Lin, F.-m. Hsu, C.-c. Lee, J.T.-S. Sun, H.-f. Yang & D.-a. Ho, 269-96. Taipei: Institute of Linguistics, Academia Sinica.

—.2005a. *Jiarongyuzu yuyan de yingao: liangge gean yanjiu (Pitch in the rGyalrongic subgroup: two case studies).* Yuyan Yanjiu 25.50-59.

—.2005b. *Linguistic coding of generic human arguments in rGyalrongic languages.* Paper presented to the the 11th Himalayan Languages Symposium 6-9 December 2005, Chulalongkorn University, Bankok, Thailand, 2005b.

—.2007b. Caodeng Jiarongyude guanxiju (Relative clauses in Caodeng rGyalrong). *Language and Linguistics* 7.905-33.

—.2007c. "Tonality in Caodeng rGyalrong." *Chomolangma, Demawend und Kasbe: Festschrift fur Roland Bielmeier zu Seinem 65 Geburtstag*, ed. by B. Huber, Marianne Volkart, and Paul Widmer, 257-80. Berlin: Mouton de Gruyter.

—.2008. "Tonality in Caodeng rGyalrong." *Chomolangma,*

Demawend und Kasbe: Festschrift fur Roland Bielmeier zu Seinem 65 Geburtstag, ed. by B. Huber, Marianne Volkart, and Paul Widmer, 257-80. Berlin: Mouton de Gruyter.

Sun, Jackson T.-S. and Shih, Danluo. 2002. "Caodeng Jiarongyu yu rentongdengdi xiangguande yufaxianxiang (Related grammatical phenomena of empathy hierarchy in Caodeng rGyalrong)." *Language and Linguistics* 3.79-99.

Sun, Jackson T.-S. & You-Jing Lin. 2007. *Constructional variation in rGyalrong relativization: how to make a choice?* Paper presented to the The International Workshop on Relative Clauses, Institute of Linguistics, Academia Sinica, Taipei, 2007.

Tao, Hongyin. 1996. *Units in Mandarin Conversation: Prosody, Discourse, and Grammar Amsterdam and Philadelphia:* John Benjamins.

Tian, Qianzi & Jackson T.-S Sun. 2016a. "Gexihuo'eryu dongci yichongdiefangshi tixiande shubiaoji (Reduplication as a device for number marking in Gexi Horpa) (in Chinese)." *Journal of Yunnan Normal University* 45.19.

—. 2016b. "Xibu Huo'eryu dongcide ciganjiaoti (Stem alternation of Western Horpa verbs) (in Chinese)." *Minzu Yuwen* 3.9.

Venditti, Jennifer J. 2005. "The J_ToBI model of Japanese intonation." *Prosodic Typology: The Phonology of Intonation and Phrasing*, ed. by S.-A. Jun, 172-200. New York: Oxford University Press.

Voeltz, Erhard F.K. & Christa Kilian-Hatz. 2001. *Introduction.* Ideophones, 1-7. Amsterdam.

Voorhoeve, Jan. 1973. Safwa as a restricted tone system. *Studies in African Linguistics* 4.1-21.

Watanabe, Yasuko. 1994. "Clause-chaining, switch-reference and action/event continuity in Japanese discourse: The case of *te*, *to*, and zero-conjunction." *Studies in Language* 18.127-203.

Wei, Jie-Wu. 2001. *Verbal Prefixation in (Zhoukeji) rGyalrong: The Problem of kɐ-/ka- Alternation:* National Tsing Hua University MA Thesis.

Wennerstrom, Ann K. 2001. *The Music of Everyday Speech.* New York: Oxford University Press.

Wong, Wai Yi P., Majorie K. M. Chan & Mary E. Beckman. 2005. "An autosegmental-metrical analysis and prosodic annotation conventions for Cantonese." *Prosodic Typology: The Phonology of Intonation and Phrasing*, ed. by S.-A. Jun, 271-300. New York: Oxford University Press.

Yip, Moira. 2002. *Tone.* Cambridge (UK): Cambridge University Press.

Zhang, Jie. 2002. *The Effects of Duration and Sonority on Contour Tone Distribution: A Typological Survey and Formal Analysis.* New York: Routledge.

Zhang, Shuya. 2016. *La phonologie et al morphologie du dialecte de Brag-dbar du Rgyalrong Situ.*

Appendix: Three Cogtse Narratives

The present appendix includes three of the twenty Cogtse narratives the present study is based on. The reader is referred to Table 1.3 for related information about all the twenty narratives.

The narratives are fully analyzed morphologically, and are transcribed with prosodic notations. The transcription applies a three-layered model. The speech is parsed into IUs. Each numbered line starts a new IU, with each IU analyzed in three layers. Layer 1 is prosodic and phonemic; Layer 2 is for morphological and phonological (especially tonal) notations; and Layer 3 provides morpheme-by- morpheme glossing. For more details of the transcription system for Rgyalrong, the reader is referred to § 4.1.2. The texts in italics are free translations of IUs or batches of IUs.

Narrative 01: Fish in Burnt Water

1 {kə^sce=jmənaŋorə=}/

    kəscêj   =mənaŋorə
    in.the.past   =TOP

2 ...(.8) {arəglə^mbɐ= kɐtsəs}

    arəkləmbê̂   kɐ-   tsâs
    Araglam.people NMZL:GP- say1

3 ... {kə^sa=m nakədo nəŋo}

kəsâm	na-	kə-	ndô	-s	nə-	ŋos
three	IMPFV:PST-	NMZL-	there.be2	-PST	OBV-	COP1

1-3 A long tine ago, there were three Araglam people ,

4 ...(2.5) {kənədzəmbo=} {cʰas tokə^lo=ɲ ptṣe}

kə-	nədzəmbôcʰas	to-	kə-	lô	-ɲ	ptṣêrə
NMZL-	travel1	together	PFV:upward-	NMZL-	set.off2	-2/3PL	CONN:then

4 they went outing together

5 {təsniti=}/

tə-	snî	=ti
one-	day	=TOP:OBL

6 ... {mjɐn^ŋgun wumtojmənaŋo}

mjɐngûn	wə-	mtô	=j	=mənaŋorə
great.river	3SG:POSS-	rim	=LOC	=TOP

5-6 One day, by a great river,

7 {tṣʰa nakə^ta=ɲ nəŋos}

tṣʰa	na-	kə-	tâ	-ɲ	nə-	ŋos
tea	PFV:downward-	NMZL-	place2	-2/3PL	OBV-	COP1

8 ...(1.0) {tonə^zɐ=ɲwuŋkʰuj ptṣerə}

to-	nəza	-ɲ	=wəŋkʰuj	ptṣêrə
PFV:upward-	dine2	-2/3PL	=after	CONN:then

7-8 after boiling tea and having a meal,

9 .. {kənə^na=ɲti}

kə-	nənâ	-ɲ	=ti
NMZL-	rest1	-2/3PL	=TOP:OBL

9 when they were resting,

10 ...(1.9) {tərgi^təmənaŋorə}

tə-	rgi	=tə	=mənaŋorə
one-	CL	=TOP	=TOP

10 One guy:

11 ...(2.8) {ʃtə=}

ʃtə
FIL

12 ... {tətʃi wuŋguj} {tʃibjoɲetə}

tə-	tʃl	wə-	ŋgu	=j	tʃlbjo	=ɲɛ̂	=tə
N-	water	3SG:POSS-inside		=LOC	fish	=PL	=TOP

13 {katʃop ɐnɐŋorə}

ka-	tʃop	ɐ-	nɐ-	ŋôs	rə
NMZL:GP-	burn1(v.t.)	IRR-	PFV:downward-	COP1	PART

11-13 "Well, if the fish in the water are set on fire

14 ...(.9) {kətəs kə^tʃʰe=zəɲe   toktsis nəŋos}

kətə	=s	kə-	tʃʰê	zə	ɲe	to-
where	=ALLABL	3PL:INTR.-	go1	PART	PART	PFV:upward-

kə-	tsis	nə-	ŋos
NMZL-	say2	OBV-	COP1

14 where will they go?" he said.

15 ...(1.6) {wandʐitəkə}

wa-	ndʐi	=tə	=kə
3SG:POSS-	friend	=TOP	=ERG

15 His friend :

16 ...(1.2) {kətitə} {sətʃʰew je}

kəti	=tə	sə-	tʃʰê	-w		je
where:LOC	=TOP	CAUS-	go1	-TR	DM	

16 "Where could they go?

17 {ʃəkos ^to kətʰo zə= .. toktsis nəŋo }

ʃəkô	=s	tô	kə-	tʰô	zə
tree.top	=ALLABL	upward	3PL:INTR.-	go.upward1	PART

to-	kə-	tsis	nə-	ŋos
PFV:upward-	NMZL-	say2	OBV-	COP1

17 sure they will go to the top of trees" he said.

18 ...(2.3) {{mɐj tərgi}gə}

mɐj	tə-	rgi	=kə
more	one-	CL	=ERG

18 Another one:

19 ... {^hə̃}

hə̃

DM

20 ...(1.7) {kə^rgurə kəmak wəŋkʰu}

kərgu	=rə	kə-	mak	wəŋkʰu
cattle	=TOP	3PL:INTR.-	COP:NEG1	after

19-20 "Come on, they are not cattle,

21 {ʃikos ^to kətʰo ^mo= toktsis nəŋo}

ʃikô	=s	tô	kə-	tʰô	mo
tree.top	=ALLABL	upward	3PL:INTR.-	go.upward1	Q
to-		kə-		tsiş	nə-	ŋoʒ
PFV:upward-		NMZL-		say2	OBV-	COP1

21 how can they go to the top of trees?" he said.

22 ...(1.1) tʂe {tərgi nakəjok} {ŋo=s}

ptʂêrə	tə-	rgi	na-	kə-	jôk	na-
CONN:then	one-	CL	PFV:downward-	NMZL-	finish2	OBV-
ŋos						
COP1						

22 One is over.

Narrative 05 Childhood: Our dogs and hunting

1 {ŋə^ɲe ʃti=}

ŋəɲê   ʃti
1PL:EXCL   here

2 ... {roŋmbɐsɐ^tʃʰe=mənaŋorə}

roŋmbɐsɐtʃʰê   =j   =mənaŋorə
the.Rgylrong.area   =LOC   =TOP

1-2 Here in the Rgyalrong Area,

3 ...(1.1) {kə^rtsuj= ptʂerə}

kərtsû   =j   ptʂêrə
winter   =LOC   CONN:then

3 During the winter,

4 ...(1.7) {ʃʰi^kʰasto=}

ʃikʰa   =stô
woods   =upward

5 {ʃe ^ʃo kɐjʒgi kəra ŋos}/

ʃe   ʃô   kɐ-   j-   ʒgî
fire.wood   all   NMZL:INF-   go.and-   collect.and.bring.back1
kə-   râ   ŋôs
NMZL-   be.needed1   COP1

4-5 it is necessary to collect and bring back fire wood.

6 ...(1.6) ẽ=

   ẽ

   FIL

7 ... {ndzok} {kəcʰa^tsa=ɲemənaŋorə}

ndzok	kə-	cʰâ	=tsâ	=ɲê	=mənaŋorə
slightly	NMZL:SUBJ-	be.capable1	=DIM	=PL	=TOP

6-7 Those who were more capable

8 ...(1.0) ə

   ə

   FILL

9 {ʃipa kapa}/

ʃipa	ka-	pa
split-up.log	NMZL:PL-	do1

8-9 split up logs,

10 ...(1.4) {ndzok} {makcʰa^tsa=ɲemənaŋorə}

ndzok	ma-	kə-	cʰâ	=tsâ	=ɲê	=mənaŋorə
slightly	NEG1-	NMZL-	be.capable1	=DIM	=PL	=TOP

10 Those who were not so capable

11 ...(.7) ptʂerə=

ptʂêrə
CONN:then

12 ...{ ʃiˆkrək kapa ptʂerə}

ʃikrêk	ka-	pa	ptʂêrə
stick.chopping	NMZL:PL-	do1	CONN:then

11-12 chopoed sticks,

13 ...(1.4) ə=

ə
FILL

14 {ʃibje}

ʃibje
thin.branch.bunching

15 ...(.7) {wutə kapa=}/

wətə	ka-	pa
that	NMZL:PL-	do1

13-15 bunched thin branches, and so on.

16 ...(.7) ptʂe {kərtsujmənaŋo} {ʃipo kaˆta= ptʂerə}

ptʂêrə	kərtsû	=j	=mənaŋorə	ʃipo	ka-
CONN:then	winter	=LOC	=TOP	woodpile	NMZL:PL-
ta	ptʂêrə				
place2	CONN:then				

16 arranged the woods into piles during the winter,

17 ...(.8) {pətsartə} {kaplutə} {kara^ŋŋo kəra} {naŋo=s}

pətsar	=tə	ka-	plû	=tə	ka-
spring	=TOP	NMZL:OBJ-	burn1	=TOP	NMZL:INF-
raŋŋo	kə-	râ	na-	ŋôs	
prepare1	NMZL-	be.needed1	IMPFV:PST-	COP2	

17 it was necessary to prepare what to burn for spring.

18 ...(1.9) {ŋəɲe=}

ŋəɲê
1PL:EXCL

19 ...(1.2) {tətʃim ^kəwi wuŋguj nɐ^ɲijtimənaŋorə}

tə-	tʃim	kə-	wi	wə-	ŋgu	=j
1PL:POSS-	house	NMZL-	be.old1	3SG:POSS-	inside	=LOC
nɐ-	ɲî	-j	=ti	=mənaŋorə		
IMPFV:PST-	live2	-1PL	=TOP:OBL	=TOP		

18-19 When we lived at our old house,

20 {ŋɐpɐ} {tɐrwɐk kənərga} {na^ŋo= ptʂerə}

ŋɐ-	pê	tɐ- rwɐk	kə-	nərga	na-	ŋôs
1SG:POSS-	father	N- hunting	NMZL-	like1	IMPFV:PST-	COP2
ptʂêrə						
CONN:then						

20 my father liked hunting.

21 ...(1.4) {ptʂerə=}

ptʂêrə
CONN:then

22 ...(1.3) {njaŋ^ʂan kɐtsə wuʒim^kʰamtimənaŋorə}

njaŋʂan   kɐ-   tsâs wə-   ʒimkʰâm =ti
Liangshan:PLN NMZL:GP-   say1 3SG:POSS- area   =TOP:OBL
=mənaŋorə
=TOP

21-22 At a region called "Liangshan"

23 ... {ɲikʰəna} {kə^sna nəŋo ptʂerə}

ɲə-   kʰəna kə-   sna   nə-   ŋos   ptʂêrə
2/3PL:POSS-   dog   NMZL-   be.good1 OBV- COP1 CONN:then

23 the dogs there were good (i.e. of good breed)

24 ...(1.8) {ŋatsikə=}

ŋa-   tsi   =kə
1SG:POSS-   youngest.uncle   =ERG

25 ...(.8) {wutəstosto=}

wətə   =stostô
that   =upward:REDU

26 {{kʰəna te} topet}/

kʰəna   te   to-   pet
dog   one   PFV:upward-   bring2

24-26 My youngest uncle brought from there one dog up here.

27 ...(1.2) {{kʰəna wurme}mənaŋorə}

kʰəna	wə-	rmê	=mənaŋorə
dog	3SG:POSS-	name(n.)	=TOP

28 {kʰə^pu= namərmes}

kʰəpu	na-	mərme	-s
Puppy(dog.name)	IMPFV:PST-	be.named2	-PST

27-28 The dog's name is Puppy.

29 ... {kʰəmo te} {naŋos}

kʰəmô	te	na-	ŋôs
female.dog	one	IMPFV:PST-	COP2

29 She was a female dog.

30 ...(1.1) ptṣerə {wutə wukʰə^natəmənaŋorə}

ptṣêrə	wətə	wə-	kʰəna	=tə	=mənaŋorə
CONN:then	that	3SG:POSS-	dog	=TOP	=TOP

31 {{tɐrwɐkɲe}tə}

tɐ-	rwɐk	=ɲê	=tə
N-	hunting	=PL	=TOP

32 ...(.7) {maŋdẓa kəpa}/

maŋdẓâ	kə-	pa
specially	NMZL-	do1

30-32 That dog was especially good at hunting (Lit: That dog
was doing specially at hunting) ,

33 ...(.5) {kɐsɐdzətɳetə} {kəcʰa} {naŋo}

kɐ-	sɐ-	dzək	=ɳê	=tə	kə-	cʰâ
NMZL:INF-	ANTIP-	chase1	=PL	=TOP	NMZL-	be.capable1
na-	ŋôs					
IMPFV:PST-	COP2					

33 with respec to chasing she was capable.

34 ...(.6) {wuʃna kəŋɐ} {naŋos}

wə-	ʃna	kə-	ŋê	na-	ŋôs
3SG:POSS-	nose	3PL:INTR.-	be.sensitive1	IMPFV:PST-	COP2

34 Her nose was sensitive.

35 {korətə=}

korə	=tə
but	=TOP

35 However,

36 ...(.4) {wugzət kə^tsi naŋos ptʂerə}

wə-	gzət	kə-	tsî	na-	ŋôs
3SG:POSS-	build(n.)	NMZL-	be.small1	IMPFV:PST-	COP2
ptʂêrə					
CONN:then					

36 she was small in build, so...

37 ...(.8) {ptʂe} w-

ptʂêrə
CONN:then

38 ...(2.0) {{tədʐək kapa}təmənaŋo}

tə-	dʐə̂k	ka-	pa	=tə	=mənaŋorə
N-	chasing	NMZL:INF-	do1	=TOP	=TOP

39 {kəŋaplo naŋos}

kə-	ŋaplo	na-	ŋôs
NMZL-	take.longer1	IMPFV:PST-	COP2

37-39 While chasing she drew it out.

40 ...(1.1) {tete=j}

tetêj
sometimes

41 ... {caɲe} {to^dʐe=kti ʒi}

câ	=ɲê	to-	dʐə̂k	=ti	ʒi
musk.deer	=PL	PFV:upward-	chase2	=TOP:OBL	still

42 {wasni-} --

wa-	snî
3SG:POSS-	day

43 ...(1.7) e=/

e
FIL

44 {təsniphɐk} {kəpsok}

tə-	snî	-	phɐ̂k	kə-		psôk
one-	day	-	half	NMZL-		be.like1

40-44 Sometimes it would take her something like a whole day or half a day.

45 ... {wuɲe}

wəɲê
those

45 Those (situations),

46 ... {ʃikhaj wupsok} {kədʑek}

ʃikha	=j	wəpsôk	kə-	dʑɐ̂k
woods	=LOC	that.way	NMZL-	chase1

46 chasing lik that in the woods,

47 ...(1.1) ptʂerə {wuthakreŋ-} --

ptʂɐ̂rə	wə-	thakrêŋ
CONN:then	3SG:POSS-	high.speed

48 {{wuthagreŋ kəmi}tə} {ptʂerə}

wə-	thakrɐ̂ŋ	kə-	mi	=tə	ptʂɐ̂rə
3SG:POSS-	high.speed	NMZL-	there.not.be1	=TOP	CONN:then

47-48 she was not fast (Lit: she did not have high speed),

49 ...(.8) {ptʂerə=}

ptʂêrə
CONN:then

50 .. {{catə}mənaŋorə}

câ   =tə   =mənaŋorə
musk.deer   =TOP   =TOP

51 ...(.8) {kasnə^ʃiko lu=}/

ka-   s-   nə-   ʃiko   lû
NMZL:INF-   CAUS-   VLZR-   tree.top   DM

52 ... ptʂe {kasat} {lu} {{kəpsokɲeɲe}tə}

ptʂêrə   ka-   sat   lû   kə-   psôk   =ɲeɲê
CONN:then   NMZL:INF-   kill1   DM   NMZL-   be.like1   =PL:REDU
=tə
=TOP

53 {kəro makcʰa} {naŋo=s}

kə-   rô   ma-   kə-   cʰâ   na-
NMZL-   be.surplus1   NEG1-   NMZL-   be.capable1   IMPFV:PST-
ŋôʀ
COP2

49-53 so she was not capable of chasing musk deer or killing
them right there on site or somethig like that.

54 ...(1.9) ptʂerə

ptʂêrə
CONN:then

55 {mətə} {ʃikʰas katʃʰe} {kənərga}

mə̂	=tə	ʃikʰa	=s	ka-	tʃʰê	kə-	nərga
3SG	=TOP	woods	=ALLABL	NMZL:INF-	go1	NMZL-	like1

54-55 She liked to go to the woods,

56 ...(1.6) {tanap} {kam} {ruu^tu=təmənaŋorə}

ta-	nâp	kam	rə̂w-	tu	=tə	=mənaŋorə
N-	morning	door	as.soon.as-	open1	=TOP	=TOP

56 in the morning as soon as the door opened,

57 ... {ptşe} {kamkʰas} {^rəwʃut kəpa ptşe} {wuʃtʃi}

ptşêrə	kam	-	kʰâ	=s	rə̂w-	kʃut
CONN:then	door	-	mouth	=ALLABL	as.soon.as-	go.out1
	kə-		pa	ptşêrə	wə-	ʃtʃî
	NMZL-		do1	CONN:then	3SG:POSS-	self

57 she would go out of the door by herself.

58 ...(.9) ptşerə

ptşêrə
CONN:then

59 ... {ʃi^kʰas ʃo kətʃʰe naŋos}

ʃikʰa	=s	ʃô	kə-	tʃʰê	na-	ŋôs
woods	=ALLABL	usually	NMZL-	go1	IMPFV:PST-	COP2

58-59 She went to the woods a lot.

60 ...(1.1) {kəməŋkʰuj=}

kəməŋkʰuj
afterwards

61 ...(1.1) {{wapu te} nandos}

wa-	pu	=te	na-	ndô	-s
3SG:POSS-	child	=one	PFV:downward-	there.be2	-PST

60-61 Afterwards she had a child.

62 .. wapu te nandostəmənaŋorə

wa-	pu	=te	na-	ndô	-s
3SG:POSS-	child	=one	PFV:downward-	there.be2	-PST
=tə	=mənaŋorə				
=TOP	=TOP				

62 She had a child

63 ...(.9) e=

e
FIL

64 {tapu=}

ta- pu
N- child

65 ... {{kʰənapu wurme} təmənaŋorə}

kʰəna	-	pu	wə-	rmê	=tə	=mənaŋorə
dog	-	child	3SG:POSS-	name(n.)	=TOP	=TOP

66 {hwaŋ^pəɹ tokaʃimərmes naŋos}

hwaŋpəɹ	to-	ka-	sə-	mərme
(dog.name)	PFV:upward-	NMZL:GP-	CAUS-	be.named2
-s	na-	ŋôs		
-PST	IMPFV:PST-	COP2		

63-66 The puppy was called Huangber.

67 ...(1.3) ptʂe {wutə} {ndzok tokə^te=stimənaŋorə ptʂerə}

ptʂêrə	wətə	ndzok	to-	kə-	te
CONN:then	that	slightly	PFV:upward-	NMZL-	be.big2
	-s	=ti	=mənaŋorə	ptʂêrə	
	-PST	=TOP:OBL	=TOP	CONN:then	

67 When (Huangber) grew up a little bit,

68 hɐjʒi {wu^mo wapsojtə}

hajʒi	wə-	mo	wa-	psô	=j	=tə
also	3SG:POSS-	mother	3SG:POSS-	side	=LOC	=TOP

69 hɐjʒi

hajʒi
also

70 ...(.7) {tədʐekɲe} {kɐ^slɐ=p ptʂerə}

tə-	dʐêk	=ɲê	kɐ-	slêp	ptʂêrə
N-	chasing	=PL	NMZL:INF-	learn1	CONN:then

68-70 from its mother it also learned chasing,

71 .. {kɐsɐdʑekɲe} {to^cʰa=s}

kɐ-	sɐ-	dʑêk	=ɲê	to-		cʰa	-s
NMZL:INF-	ANTIP-	chase1	=PL	PFV:upward-		be.capable 2	-PST

71 then it was capable of chasing.

72 ...(1.6) {ptʂerə=}

ptʂêrə
CONN:then

73 {təpa ^ti=mənaŋorə}

tə-	pâ	=ti	=mənaŋorə
one-	year	=TOP:OBL	=TOP

72-73 One year,

74 ...(1.9) {{kərtsuʃe kapa} na-mdak}

kərtsû -	ʃe	ka-	pa na-		mdâk
winter -	fire.wood	NMZL:INF-	do1 PFV:downward-		be.time.to2

*74 Then one year, it was time to collect firewoord for the
    winter.*

75 .. {ʃeʒgiɲe kapa} {na^mdak ptʂerə}

ʃe	-	ʒgî	=ɲê	ka-	pa
fire.wood	-	collect.and.bring.back1	=PL	NMZL:INF-	do1
na-		mdâk			
PFV:downward-		be.time.to2			
ptʂêrə					
CONN:then					

75 It was time to collect and bring back firewood, so,

76 ...(.7) {ŋa nɐrə} {{ŋajandʒɐs}təmənaŋorə}

ŋa	nɐrə	ŋa-	jâ	=ndʒês
1SG	and	1SG:POSS-	older.brother.and.sister	=DU
=tə	=mənaŋorə			
=TOP	=TOP			

77 ...(1.4) {ʃe kə^pʰot toktʰɐtʃʰ_(/toktʰɐtsʰ/)} {naŋos}

ʃe	kə-	pʰôt	to-	kə-	tʰɐl	-tʃ
fire.wood	NMZL-	chop1	PFV:upward-	NMZL-	go2	-1DU
na-	ŋôs					
IMPFV:PST-	COP2					

76-77 me and my older brother went to chop firewood.

78 ...(1.2) ptʂerə

ptʂêrə
CONN:then

79 {ʃe kəpʰot} {kə^tʰotʃitimənaŋorə} ji-

ʃe	kə-	pʰôt	kə-	tʰô	-tʃ	=ti
fire.wood	NMZL-	chop1	NMZL-	go.upward1	-1DU	=TOP:OBL
=mənaŋorə						
=TOP						

78-79 When we two went upward to chop firewood,

80 ... {tanap} {kam} {toŋatuti}

ta-	nâp	kam	to-	ŋa-	tu	=ti
N-	morning	door	PFV:upward-	GP-	open2	=TOP:OBL

80 when the door opened in the morning,

81 {kʰəˆnadʒe} {nəkəˆkʃut ptʂerə}

kʰəna	=ndʒês	nə-	kə-	kʃût	ptʂêrə
dog	=DU	PFV:westwards-	NMZL-	go.out2	CONN:then

81 the two dogs would go out,

82 ... {ʃiˆkʰas taaktʃʰe}

ʃikʰa	=s	ta-	â-	kə-	tʃʰe
woods	=ALL/ABL	EVI:PFV:upward-	EVI-	NMZL-	go1

82 they went to the woods.

83 ...(2.0) {ptʂerə}

ptʂêrə
CONN:then

84 ... {ŋədʒe=} {atɐj} {tomdətʃti}

ŋədʒê	atâ	=j	to-	mdə
1DU	upward.direction	=LOC	PFV:upward-	arrive2
-tʃ	=ti			
-1DU	=TOP:OBL			

83-84 When the two of us got up there,

85 .. {{kʰənadʒe}təmənaŋorə}

kʰəna	=ndʒês	=tə	=mənaŋorə
dog	=DU	=TOP	=TOP

86 ...(1.0) ^ptʂerə=

ptʂêrə
CONN:then

87 ... {ca te}

câ   =te
musk.deer =one

88 ...{ʃikoj} {təwrko}/

ʃikô   =j   ta-   â-   w-   rko
tree.top =LOC EVI:PFV:upward- EVI- INV- contain1

85-88 the two dogs had cornered a musk deer to the top of a
tree.

89 ...(2.1) {wu^tətə hɐjʒi=}

wətətə hajʒi
FIL   still

90 .. {kəŋɐnədo^do naŋo ptʂerə}

kə-   ŋɐnədodô   na-   ŋôs   ptʂêrə
NMZL-   be.coincidental1 IMPFV:PST-   COP2 CONN:then

93 {ʃirpa te=}

ʃirpâ   -   te
ax   -   one

94 {ldu te}

ldû   =te
machete   =one

95 ...(1.2) {ptʂerə}

ptʂêrə
CONN:then

96 .. tʂoz-

97 ... {tʂoˆzon tokdzə̂ttʃitə} {wundzəs} {naˆmes wuŋkʰu}

tʂonzôn	to-	kə-	dzə̂t	-tʃ	=tə	wundzəs
field.rations	PFV:upward-	NMZL-	take2	-1DU	=TOP	no.more
na-	mê	-s	wəŋkʰu			
IMPFV:PST-	there.not.be2	-PST	after			

91-97 The two of us had nothing but an ax, a machete, and some field rations.

98 ...(1.2) {ptʂerə}

ptʂêrə
CONN:then

99 ...(1.6) {ŋatəmənaŋorə}

Ŋa	=tə	=mənaŋorə
1SG	=TOP	=TOP

100 ... {ndzok} {kəˆcʰa=ŋtəmənaŋo ptʂerə}

ndzok	kə-	cʰâ	-ŋ	=tə	=mənaŋorə	ptʂêrə
slightly	NMZL-	be.capable1	-1SG	=TOP	=TOP	CONN:then

98-100 I was a little more capable.

101 ... {ʃikos ˆto totʰɐŋ ptʂerə}

ʃikô	=stô	to-	tʰɐl	-ŋ	ptʂêrə
tree.top	=upward	PFV:upward-	go2	-1SG	CONN:then

101 So I climbed up to the top of the tree.

102 ... {ŋəʒode} {nəskʰen}

ŋə-	ʒode	na-	skʰêt	-ŋ
1SG:POSS-	puttee	PFV:downward-	take.out2	-1SG

102 I took off my puttee.

103 ...(1.1) {ptʂe} {ŋəldutʰoktə} wu-

ptʂêrə	ŋə-	ldû	-	tʰôk	=tə
CONN:then	1SG:POSS-	machete	-	sheath	=TOP

104 ... {wutə wa^spraktə nəskʰen ptʂerə}

wətə	wa-	sprâk	=tə	na-	skʰêt
that	3SG:POSS-	belt	=TOP	PFV:downward-	take.out2

-ŋ	ptʂêrə
-1SG	CONN:then

103-104 and I took off the belt of the sheath of my machete.

105 ...(.7) {tɐkpok to^pɐŋ ptʂerə}

tɐ-	kpok	to-	pê	-ŋ	ptʂêrə
N-	noose	PFV:upward-	do2	-1SG	CONN:then

105 I made a noose.

106 ... ^ptʂe=

ptʂêrə
CONN:then

107 ...(.7) {ca wumki} {natsʰiktʃʰ_(/natsʰikts/)}

câ	wə-	mkî	na-	tsʰîk	-tʃ
musk.deer	3SG:POSS-	neck	PFV:downward-	string.up(v.t.)2	-1DU

106-107 Then we strung up the musk deer.

108 ... {wutimənaŋorə}

wəti	=mənaŋorə
there	=TOP

109 ...(1.1) e=

e
FIL

110 catə=

câ	=tə
musk.deer	=TOP

111 {nasattʃʰ_(/nasattsʰ/)}

na-	sât	-tʃ
PFV:downward-	kill2	-1DU

108-111 We two killed the musk deer

112 ... {^ptʂerə=}

ptʂêrə
CONN:then

113 ...(1.7) {ca^ɲe}

câ	=ɲê
musk.deer	=PL

114 ... {nasatts wu^ŋkʰu=j ptʂe}

na-	sât	-tʃ	wəŋkʰu	ptʂêrə
PFV:downward-	kill2	-1DU	after	CONN:then

112-114 After we killed the musk deer

115 ...(.7) {^ptʂe ʃe kə^pʰot to^tʰɐ=ltʃʰ_(/totʰɐ=ltsʰ/)}

ptʂêrə	ʃe	kə-	pʰôt	to-	tʰɐl	-tʃ
CONN:then	fire.wood	NMZL-	chop1	PFV:upward-	go2	-1DU

115 We went to chop firewood.

116 ...(1.1) {ʃeɲe=}

ʃe	=ɲê
fire.wood	=PL

117 {təsni} {napʰotʃʰ_(/napotsə/)}

tə-	snî	na-	pʰôt	-tʃ
one-	day	PFV:downward-	chop2	-1DU

116-117 We cut firewood for the whole day.

118 ... {təmor} {ptʂe} {jinəjɐjmənaŋorə}

tə-	mor	ptʂêrə	jə-	nəjâ	-j	=mənaŋorə
N-	night	CONN:then	PFV-	go.home2	-1PL	=TOP

119 ...(.7) {dʒikanaktʂuttəmənaŋorə}

dʒə-	ka-	naktʂut	=tə	=mənaŋorə
1DU:POSS-	NMZL:OBJ-	also.bring.on.the.way1	=TOP	=TOP

120 {^cateɲe} {nandos}

câ	teɲê	na-	ndô	-s
musk.deer	those	IMPFV:PST-	there.be2	-PST

118-120 We we went home at night, we had the musk deer to take along home.

121 ...(1.3) {ptʂerə}

ptʂêrə
CONN:then

122 ...(1.1) {caʃatəmənaŋorə} {təmor} {ptʂerə}

câ	- ʃâ	=tə	=mənaŋorə	tə-	mor	ptʂêrə
musk.deer	- flesh	=TOP	=TOP	N-	night	CONN:then

123 ... {jaŋju ^cʰastə}

Jaŋju	cʰas	=tə
Potato	together	=TOP

124 ...(2.5) {jizɐmtʰɐm} {ko^pɐj ptʂerə}

jə-	zɐmtʰɐm	ko-	pê	-j	ptʂêrə
1PL:POSS-	meal	PFV:eastwards-	make2	-1PL	CONN:then

121-124 At night, we made a dish of the musk deer meat with potatoes.

125 {təmortəmənaŋorə} {wutətə}

tə-	mor	=tə	=mənaŋorə	wətətə
N-	night	=TOP	=TOP	FIL

126 .. {japri}

ja-	pri
1PL:POSS-	supper

127 .. {ca^ʃaɲe kaza} {nandos}

câ	-	ʃâ	=ɲê	ka-	za	na-
musk.deer	-	flesh	=PL	NMZL:GP-	eat1	PFV:downward-
ndô		-s				
there.be2		-PST				

125-127 At night, we had musk deer meat for dinner.

128 ...(1.5) {tomes}

to-	mê	-s
PFV:upward-	there.not.be2	-PST

128 That was it (Lit. There is no more).

Narrative 20 The King who Punished a River

1 {mɐju=}

mɐju
more

2 {mɐju tə^rgi=təmənaŋorə}

mɐju	tə-	rgi	=tə	=mənaŋorə
more	one-	CL	=TOP	=TOP

1-2 And, still one more

3 ...(1.1) <PAR tʰəke mərme PAR>

tʰəke	mərmê
what	be.named1

3 What is it...

4 ...(.7) e

e
FIL

5 ... <PAR ana te nagdontʃ nəŋo PAR> /\

ana	te	na-	kə-	ndô	-ntʃ	nə-	ŋos
FILL	PART	IMPFV:PST-	NMZL-	there.be2	-2/3DU	OBV-	COP1

4-5 There were two.

6 ... ma {rɟɐl^po wumitə pre} tʃimtə-

mɐju	rɟɐlpö	wə-	mi	=tə	ptʂêrə
more	king	3SG:POSS-	daughter	=TOP	CONN:then

6 also a king's daughter

7 {mɐju} {rɟɐlpo ^te= nɐgdos nəŋo}

mɐju	rɟɐlpô	te	na-	kə-	ndô	-s
more	king	one	IMPFV:PST-	NMZL-	there.be2	-PST
nə-	ŋos					
OBV-	COP1					

7 There was another king.

8 {^wtət kəmak ^te= naŋŋo nəŋo}

wətətə	kə-	mak	te	na-	kə-	ŋôs
FIL	NMZL-	COP:NEG1	one	IMPFV:PST-	NMZL-	COP2

nə-	ŋos
OBV-	COP1

8 Not that one, it was another one.

9 ... {pre} {wtə wurɟɐlpotəmənaŋorə}

ptṣêrə	wətə	wə-	rɟɐlpô	=tə	=mənaŋorə
CONN:then	that	3SG:POSS-	king	=TOP	=TOP

10 {wumi kənə^rga ^jo= kɐtsə ma^ŋgɐj ji naŋŋos nəŋo}

wə-	mi	kə-	nərga	jo	kɐtsəs
3SG:POSS-	daughter	NMZL-	like1	DM	DM:EMPH
ma-	kə-	ŋgêj	te	na-	kə-
NEG1-	NMZL-	be.the.same1	PART	IMPFV:PST-	NMZL-
ŋôs	nə-	ŋos			
COP2	OBV-	COP1			

9-10 The king liked his daughter very much.

11 ... {tə^sniti pre} {wumitə} {tʃimtozna=}

tə-	snî	=ti	ptṣêrə	wə-	mi	=tə
one-	day	=TOP:OBL	CONN:then	3SG:POSS-	daughter	=TOP
tʃi	-	mtô	=snâ			
water	-	rim	=upward			

12 {kə^mbri naatʃʰe nəŋo}/

kə-	mbrî	na-	â-	tʃʰe	nə-	ŋos
NMZL-	play1	EVI:IMPFV:PST-	EVI-	go2	OBV-	COP1

11-12 One day, his daugher when to play at the riverside.

13 ... {tʃimtoj} {jaatʃʰe} {kə^mbri jaatʃʰeti}

tʃi	-	mtô	=j	ja-	â-	tʃʰe	kə-
water	-	rim	=LOC	EVI:PFV-	EVI-	go2	NMZL-
mbrî	ja-	â-	tʃʰe	=ti			
play1	EVI:PFV-	EVI-	go2	=TOP:OBL			

13 She went to the riverside, and when she went and played at the riverside,

14 prerə {tətʃikə} {jaatsam}/

ptṣêrə	tə-	tʃi	=kə	ja-	â-	tsam
CONN:then	N-	water	=ERG	EVI:PFV-	EVI-	take.away1

14 the water took her away.

15 ...(.8) {tətʃikə} {jaatsam} {pre} {ɹɐlporə} {tənəsu^su= wji}

tə-	tʃi	=kə	ja-	â-	tsam	ptṣêrə
N-	water	=ERG	EVI:PFV-	EVI-	take.away1	CONN:then
ɹɐlpô	=rə	tə-	nəsusu	wuji		
king	=TOP	NMZL-	be.sad2	PART		

15 The water took (her) away, and the king was so very sad.

16 {təkʰɐz} {^wji kə} {wuspogɲe=}

tə-   kʰɐs   wuji   =kə   wə-   spok
NMZL- lose.one's.temper2 PART =INST 3SG:POSS- beneath(n.)
=ɲê
=PL

17 {{tarorɈɐplon ɲiwɐj}kə}

ta- ro - Ɉɐplôn ɲə-   wâ   =j   =kə
N- leader - minister 2/3PL:POSS- whereabout =LOC =ERG

16-17 Enraged, to the leader ministers beneath him he said,

18 ... {kʰəncʰamɲe} ŋə- --

kʰəncʰam   =ɲê
DM:damn.it   =PL

19 {{ŋəmirə} wɐstorəro} {məŋatpɐɲ}/

ŋə-   mi   =rə   wɐsto - rərô   mâ-   ŋa-
1SG:POSS- daughter =TOP   most - take.care1 NEG2:EVI- GP-
tə-   pɐ   -ɲ
2-   do1   -2/3PL

18-19 "Damn it, you did not take good are of my daughter,

20 {tətʃikə} {jaatsʰə^tsɐɲ} {prerə} {{ŋəmitə}rə}

tə-   tʃi   =kə   ja-   â-   tə-   sə-
N-   water =ERG   EVI:PFV- EVI-   2-   CAUS-
tsam   -ɲ   ptṣêrə   ŋə-   mi   =tə   =rə
take.away1 -2/3PL CONN:then 1SG:POSS- daughter =TO P =TOP

20 and let the river took my daughter away,

21 ... ana ʃtə {mjɐnguntəmənaŋorə}/

ana	ʃtə	mjɐngûn	=tə	=mənaŋorə
FILL	this	great.river	=TOP	=TOP

22 {təsniti} {nɐjnɐtɐr}/

tə-	snî	=ti	nɐ-	j-	nɐtɐr	-ɲ
one-	day	=TOP:OBL	IMP:downward-	go.and-	strike1	-2/3PL

21-22 Go you all and strik the river for a day.

*23 ... {stoŋˆsni kɐjnɐtɐr}_*

stoŋsnî	kɐ-	j-	nɐtɐr
every.day	NMZL:INF-	go.and-	strike1

23 Going to strike every day,

24 .. ə

ə
FILL

25 ... {ʃɐmbrə} {toˆdʐin ptʂerə}

ʃɐmbrə̂	to-	dʐə̂t	-ɲ	ptʂêrə
iron.chain	IMP-	take1	-2/3PL	CONN:then

25 take the iron chain with you

26 {nɐ^nɐtɐɲ ptʂerə}/

nɐ-	nɐtɐr	-ɲ	ptʂêrə
IMP:downward-	strike1	-2/3PL	CONN:then

26 and strike

27 ... {ŋəmitə} {tətʃi ka^tsamtə}

ŋə-	mi	=tə	tə-	tʃi	ka-	tsam
1SG:POSS-	daughter	=TOP	N-	water	NMZL:INF-	take.away1
=tə						
=TOP						

27 My daughter , the river took her

28 ə- ə- {wu^kʰaj katsamtəmənaŋorə}/

ə	ə	wə-	kʰâ	=j	ka-	tsam
FILL	FILL	3SG:POSS-	mouth	=LOC	NMZL:INF-	take.away1
=tə	=mənaŋorə					
=TOP	=TOP					

28 Took her into the water,

29 {nɐwɐtʃɐŋ te}

nɐ-	wɐtʃɐ̃	-ŋ	te
PFV:downward-	be.responsible2	-1SG	one

30 ... {mjɐngunkə mɐ^tsə mitəmənaorə}/

mjɐngûn	=kə	mɐ-	tsâs	mi	=tə	=mənaŋorə
great.river	=ERG	NEG1-	say1	there.not.be1	=TOP	=TOP

29-30 until the water says "I am responsible",

31 {snirikə}

> snirî   kə
> every.day   PART

32 {rɟɐplonɲe}

> rɟɐplôn   =ɲê
> minister =PL

33 ... e

> e
> FIL

34 {mjɐngun kəjnɐtɐr} {kəra ^ŋo= taatsə}

mjɐngûn	kɐ-	j-	nɐtɐr	kə-
great.river	NMZL:INF-	go.and-	strike1	NMZL-
râ	ŋôs	ta-	â-	tsəs
be.needed2	COP1	EVI:PFV:upward-	EVI-	say1

31-34 the ministers have to go and strike the river every day."

35 ...(1.8) ptşerə/

> ptşêrə
> CONN:then

36 {təsni rɟɐ^plon tərgi=}_

> tə-   snî   rɟɐplôn tə-   rgi
> one-   day   minister one-   CL

37 ... {tətʃĩ kʰɐj} {na}_

tə-	tʃĩ	-	kʰâ	=j	nâ
N-	water	-	mouth	=LOC	downwards

38 {ʃɐ^mbrə wurca} {^ʃpə=ktə ʃpək ʃo}

ʃɐmbrâ	wərca	ʃpək	=tə	ʃpək
iron.chain	DM:that.way	ONOM:crack!	=TOP	ONOM:crack!
ʃô	kɐ-	lêt		
always	NMZL:INF-	release1		

*35-38 So each day one minister would use the iron chain and
go crack! crack! whipping into the water.*

39 {wasni} {wutə^ksə ʃo}

wa-	snî	wətəksân	ʃô
3SG:POSS-	day	that.way	all

39 The whole day

40 ... {təsni tə^rgi= tərgi wutəksə ʃo}

tə-	snî	tə-	rgi	tə-	rgi	wətəksân	ʃô
one-	day	one-	CL	one-	CL	that.way	always

40 one (person) a day

41 ... wukə- tə- {mjɐngun kənɐ^tɐ=r kɐji nagraz nəŋo}

mjɐngûn	kə-	nɐtɐr	kɐ-	jî		
great.river	NMZL-	strike1	NMZL:INF-	go.down1		
na-	kə-	râ	-s	nə-	ŋos
IMPFV:PST-	NMZL-	be.needed2	-PST	OBV-	COP1

41 they had to go down and strike the river.

42 ... {ptʂe} {wutəksə} ji-

ptʂêrə   wətəksên
CONN:then   that.way

43 {ʃjatʃʰytə=}

ʃjatʃʰy   =tə
go.down(Chinese.loan)   =TOP

42-43 They just went down like that

44 {kolo=} wuʒi

Kolo   wuʒi
after(Chinese.loan)   PART

45 {toŋnəˆsni wji nɐktʰɐl nəŋo}

toŋnə̂ - snî wuji   nɐ-   kə-   tʰɐl nə-   ŋos
several - day PART   PFV:downward- NMZL- go2 OBV-   COP1

44-45 After several days passed,

46 ... {kəməŋkʰutə} {mɐju} {rɹɐblɐn} {mɐju} {təˆrgi=} .. kə

kəməŋkʰu =tə   mɐju rɹɐplôn   mɐju tə-   rgi =kə
afterwards =TOP more minister more one-   CL   =ERG

47 {kɐji wuˆʃez jikpi nəŋo}

kɐ-   jî   wə-   ʃes   jə-   kə-
NMZL:OBJ-   go.down1 3SG:POSS-   shift(n.) PFV- NMZL-
pi   nə-   ŋos
come2   OBV-   COP1

46-47 again it was another minister's turn to go down (to the river).

48 ... {wutə tə}

wətətə
FIL

49 tʃim- e-

50 {tʃimtoj} {namdu_(/namdə/)ti_(/tə/)} {prerə}

tʃi   - mtô =j   na-   mdu   =ti
water   - rim =LOC PFV:downward- arrive2 =TOP:OBL
ptṣêrə
CONN:then

50 When he arrived at the riverside,

51 ...(.7) ptṣe {tʃimtoj} {re=j}

ptṣêrə   tʃi - mtô =j   rê
CONN:then water- rim =LOC downstream

52 {ku te} {ᶺdi teɲe jaatʃʰe}

kû   =te   dî   =te   =ɲê   ja-   â-   tʃʰe
eastwards =one westwards =one =PL EVI:PFV- EVI- go1

51-52 he weent up and down along the river.

53 {pre wusə^soj te jaapo pre} m/

ptʂêrə	wə-	səsô	=j	te	ja-	â-
CONN:then	3SG:POSS-	thought(n.)	=LOC	one	EVI:PFV-	EVI-
po	ptʂêrə	m				
come1	CONN:then	FIL				

54 {^/m...(.7) taatsətə}/

ta-	â-	tsəs	=tə
N-	EVI-	say1	=TOP

53-54 Then he got an idea, so he said "Mm!"

55 {pre} {kəmə^ŋkʰutə pre}

ptʂêrə	kəməŋkʰu	=tə	ptʂêrə
CONN:then	afterwards	=TOP	CONN:then

56 {taapo}/

ta-	â-	po
N-	EVI-	come1

55-56 Then he came up.

57 {rɟɐlpo wɐj}

rɟɐlpô	wə-	wâ	=j
king	3SG:POSS-	whereabout	=LOC

57 To the king:

58 ... rɟɐ- ŋəpuɲe/

ŋə-	pû	=ɲê
1SG:POSS-	master	=PL

59 .. {məsnirə} {tətʃi} {nɐnɐ^tɐŋr korə}_

məsni	=rə	tə-	tʃi	nɐ-	nɐtêr	-ŋ	korə
today	=TOP	N-	water	PFV:downward-	strike2	-1SG	but

58-59   "My lord, I stroke the river today, but"

60 ... {tətʃikə=}

tə-	tʃi	=kə
N-	water	=ERG

60 the river said:

61 .. kə {ʃtətə}

kə	ʃtə	=tə
PART	this	=TOP

62 {nəmi kə^tsamtəmənao}

nə-	mi	kə-	tsam	=tə	=mənaŋorə
2SG:POSS-	daughter	NMZL:SUBJ-	take.away1	=TOP	=TOP

63 {kə^sce nəktʰɐlɲe} {kə^ŋo zə}_

kə-	scê	nə-	kə-	tʰɐl	=ɲê
NMZL:SUBJ-	be.in.the.front1	PFV:westwards-	NMZL-	go2	=PL
kə-	ŋôs				
3PL:INTR.-	COP1				
zə					
PART					

62-63 "Well... what took your daughter was (the water) that went down ahead.

64 {ŋəˆɲeʃtə} {{kəməŋkʰuɲe}rə}/

ŋəɲê	ʃtə	kə-	məŋkʰu	=ɲê	=rə
1PL:EXCL	this	NMZL:SUBJ-	be.in.the.back1	=PL	=TOP

64 We the ones that came after

65 ... {ʃimoŋmok jiˆpə=j wuŋkʰurə}

ʃimokmok	jə-	pi	-j	wəŋkʰurə
just.now:REDU	PFV-	come2	-1PL	afterwards

65 just got here just now so

66 {prerə} {ŋəɲetə} {mɐwɐtʃɐj}/

ptsêrə	ŋəɲê	=tə	mɐ-	wɐtʃɐ	-j
CONN:then	1PL:EXCL	=TOP	NEG1-	be.responsible1	-1PL

66 we are not responsible.

67 ... {nɐgwɐtʃɐstəmənao}

nɐ-	kə-	wɐtʃɐ̃	-s	=tə	=mənaŋorə
PFV:downward-	NMZL-	be.responsible2	-PST	=TOP	=TOP

68 {kəˆsceɲe} {naŋˆŋo= nɐkˆtsə=s wuŋkʰurə}

kə-	scê	=ɲê	na-	kə-	ŋôs
NMZL:SUBJ-	be.in.the.front1	=PL	IMPFV:PST-	NMZL-	COP2
nɐ-	kə-			tsəs	wəŋkʰurə
OBV-	NMZL-			say1	afterwards

*67-68 The responsible ones were the ones that went ahead' they
said.*

69 ... {wutə te=}\

wətə	te
that	one

70 {topotasə^mtso=ɲ toktsis nəŋo}

to-	po-	ta-	səmtsô	-ɲ	to-
PFV:upward-	come.and-	1SUBJ:2OBJ-	report2	-2/3PL	PFV:upward-
kə-	tsis	nə-	ŋos		
NMZL-	say2	OBV-	COP1		

69-70 that's what I came to report to you" said (the minister).

71 ... {ptşe} {wutitə} {rɟɐlpo} {tʰək^tʰə=k tərzəkɲe naaɲi}

ptşêrə	wəti	=tə	rɟɐlpô	tʰəktʰək	tə-	rzək	=ɲê
CONN:then	at.that.time	=TOP	king	IDE	one-	length	=PL
na-	â-	ɲi					
EVI:PFV-	EVI-	ponder1					

71 Then, at that time, the king pondered it for a while.

72 ... a {wutə} {ʒi} {nawasu}/

A	wətə	ʒi	na-	wasu
Ah	that	also	OBV-	be.correct1

72 "Ah, that's quite right

73 {{ŋəmi kətsam}tə}_

ŋə-	mi	kə-	tsam	=tə
1SG:POSS-	there.not.be1	NMZL:SUBJ-	take.away1	=TOP

74 {kəsce} {tə^tʃi nəkpiɲe nɐikəŋo}_

kə-	scê	tə-	tʃi		nə-
NMZL-	be.in.the.front1	N-	water		PFV:westwards-
kə-	pi		=ɲê	nɐî-	kə-
NMZL-	come2		=PL	EVI:IMPFV:PST-	NMZL-
ŋos					
COP1					

73-74 What took my daughter were the waters that came ahead.

75 .. {{kəməŋkʰuɲe}tərə} {ɲɐtʃɐ te} {mi} {nə^ŋo= wuŋkʰurə}

kə-	məŋkʰu	=ɲê	=tə		=rə
NMZL:SUBJ-	be.in.the.back1	=PL	=TOP		=TOP
ɲɐ-	tʃɐ̂		te	mi	nə- ŋos
2/3PL:POSS-	responsibility		one	there.not.be1	OBV-COP
wəŋkʰurə					
afterwards					

75 The ones that came afterwards are not responsible.

76 ... {sosni ^stɐs prerə}

sôsni	-	stɐ̂s	ptʂêrə
tomorrow	-	from	CONN:then

77 {mjɐngun kɐjnɐtɐr} {wu^dzi kəra ^mi= taatsəs prerə}

mjɐngûn	kɐ-	j-	nɐtɐr	wundzəs
great.river	NMZL:INF-	go.and-	strike1	no.more
kə-	râ	mi	ta-	â-
NMZL-	be.needed1	there.not.be1	EVI:PFV:upward-	EVI-
tsəs	ptʂêrə			
say1	CONN:then			

76-77 From tomorrow on, it is not necessary to go and strike the river" said (the king).

78 ...(1.0) {wuti=}

wəti
there

79 ... {wuti} {na ^te= naakʃin nəŋo}

wəti	nâ	te	na-	â-	kʃin	nə-	ŋos
there	downwards	PART	EVI:IMPFV:PST-EVI-		finish1	OBV-	COP1

78-79 It's over here.